TABLE of CONTENTS

Multiple Intelligences

GRADE 4

teaching kids the way they learn

written by
M.C. Hall

Cover by Dawn Devries Sokol
Interior illustrations by Kay McCabe and Kelly McMahon
Symbol design by Rose Sheifer

FS-23283 Multiple Intelligences: Teaching Kids the Way They Learn Grade 4
All rights reserved. Printed in the U.S.A.
Copyright © 1999 Frank Schaffer Publications, Inc.
23740 Hawthorne Blvd., Torrance, CA 90505

What Is the Multiple Intelligences Theory?

The Multiple Intelligences Theory, developed and researched by Dr. Howard Gardner, recognizes the multifaceted profile of the human mind. In his book *Frames of Mind* (Basic Books, 1993) Dr. Gardner explains that every human possesses several intelligences in greater or lesser degrees. Each person is born with a unique intelligence profile and uses any or all of these intelligences to acquire knowledge and experience.

At present Gardner has defined eight intelligences. Below are the intelligences and a simplified definition of each. A more complete explanation of each intelligence is found at the end of the introduction.

- verbal-linguistic: word intelligence
- logical-mathematical: number and reasoning intelligence
- visual-spatial: picture intelligence
- musical-rhythmic: music and rhythm intelligence
- bodily-kinesthetic: body intelligence
- interpersonal: social intelligence
- intrapersonal: self intelligence
- naturalist: natural environment intelligence

Gardner stresses that although intelligence is a biological function, it is inseparable from the cultural context in which it exists. He cites the example of Bobby Fischer, the chess champion. In a culture without chess, Fischer would not have been able to become a good chess player.

The Multiple Intelligences Theory in the Classroom

The Multiple Intelligences Theory has been making its way into the educational setting over the past decade. Instinctively, educators have recognized that their students learn differently, respond uniquely to a variety of teaching techniques, and have their individual preferences. Traditional educational programs do not recognize the unique intelligence profile of each student. Traditionally educators have operated according to the belief that there is a single type of intelligence, based on a combination of math and verbal ability. This more one-dimensional view gave rise to the commonly held definition of an "IQ." According to this definition, all individuals are born with this general ability and it does not change with age, training, or experience. Dr. Gardner's theory plays a significant role in rethinking how to educate so as to meet each student's individual needs. Basic skills can be more effectively acquired if all of a student's strengths are involved in the learning process.

The key to lesson design for a multiple intelligences learning environment is to reflect on the concept you want to teach and identify the intelligences that seem most appropriate for communicating the content. At Mountlake Terrace High School in Edmonds, Washington, Eeva Reeder's math students learn about algebraic equations kinesthetically by using the pavement in the school's yard like a giant graph. Using the large, square cement blocks of the pavement, they identify the axes, the X and Y coordinates, and plot themselves as points on the axes.

Other teachers will attempt to engage all eight intelligences in their lessons by using learning centers to focus on different approaches to the same concept. An example of this is Bruce Campbell's third grade classroom in Marysville, Washington. Campbell, a consultant on teaching through multiple intelligences, has designed a unit on Planet Earth that includes seven centers: a building center where students use clay to make models of the earth; a math center; a reading center; a music center where students study unit spelling words while listening to music; an art center using concentric circle patterns; a cooperative learning activity; a writing center titled, "Things I would take with me on a journey to the center of the earth."

Another way to use the multiple intelligences theory in the classroom is through student projects. For example, Barbara Hoffman had her third-grade students in Country Day School in Costa Rica develop games in small groups. The students had to determine the objective and rules of the game. They researched questions and answers and designed and assembled a game board and accessories. Many intelligences were engaged through the creation of this project.

Dr. Gardner recommends that schools personalize their programs by providing apprenticeships. These should be designed to allow students to pursue their interests, with an emphasis on acquiring expertise over a period of time. In the Escuela Internacional Valle del Sol in Costa Rica, apprenticeships based on the eight intelligences are used. In one program long-term special subjects are offered to students in areas such as cooking, soccer, and drama. In addition, at the end of the term the entire school participates in a special project in multiage grouping with activities focused around a theme such as Egypt or European medieval life.

Assessment

The multiple intelligences theory challenges us to redefine assessment and see it as an integral part of the learning process. Dr. Gardner believes that many of the intelligences do not lend themselves to being measured by standardized paper and pencil tests. In a classroom structured on the multiple intelligences theory, assessment is integrated with learning and instruction and stimulates further learning. The teacher, the student, and his or her peers are involved in ongoing assessment. In this way the student has a better understanding of his or her strengths and weaknesses. Self-evaluation gives students the opportunity to set goals, to use higher-order thinking skills, as well as to generalize and personalize what they learn.

One example of nontraditional assessment is the development and maintenance of student portfolios, including drafts, sketches, and final products. Both student and teacher choose pieces that illustrate the student's growth. (Gardner calls these process folios.) Self-assessment can also include parental assessment, as well as watching video-taped student performances, and students editing or reviewing each other's work.

How to Use This Book

Multiple Intelligences: Teaching Kids the Way They Learn is designed to assist teachers in implementing this theory across the curriculum. This book is for teachers of students in fourth grade. It is divided into six subject areas: language arts, social studies, mathematics, science, fine arts, and physical education. Each subject area offers a collection of practical, creative ideas for teaching each of the eight intelligences. The book also offers reproducible student worksheets to supplement many of these activities. (A small image of the worksheet can be found next to the activity it supplements. Answers are provided at the end of the book.) Teachers may pick and choose from the various activities to develop a multiple intelligences program that meets their students' needs.

The activities are designed to help the teacher engage all the intelligences during the learning process so that the unique qualities of each student are recognized, encouraged, and cultivated. The activities provide opportunities for students to explore their individual interests and talents while learning the basic knowledge and skills that all must master. Each activity focuses on one intelligence; however, other intelligences will come into play since the intelligences naturally interact with each other.

As a teacher, you have the opportunity to provide a variety of educational experiences that can help students excel in their studies as well as discover new and exciting abilities and strengths within themselves. Your role in the learning process can provide students with an invaluable opportunity to fulfill their potential and enrich their lives.

Words of Advice

The following are some tips to assist you in using the Multiple Intelligences Theory in your classroom.

- Examine your own strengths and weaknesses in each of the intelligences. Call on others to help you expand your lessons to address the entire range of intelligences.

- Spend time in the early weeks of the school year working with your students to evaluate their comfort and proficiency within the various intelligences. Use your knowledge of their strengths to design and implement your teaching strategies.

- Refrain from "pigeonholing" your students into limited areas of intelligence. Realize that a student can grow from an activity that is not stressing his or her dominant intelligence.

- Work on goal-setting with students and help them develop plans to attain their goals.

- Develop a variety of assessment strategies and record-keeping tools.

- Flexibility is essential. The Multiple Intelligences Theory can be applied in a myriad of ways. There is no one right way.

The Eight Intelligences

Below is a brief definition of each of the eight intelligences, along with tips on how to recognize the characteristics of each and how to develop these intelligences in your students.

Verbal-Linguistic Intelligence

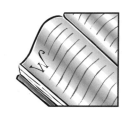

Verbal-linguistic intelligence consists of:

- a sensitivity to semantics—the meaning of words
- a sensitivity to syntax—the order among words
- a sensitivity to phonology—the sounds, rhythms, and inflections of words
- a sensitivity to the different functions of language, including its potential to excite, convince, stimulate, convey information, or please

Verbal-linguistic intelligence consists of the ability to think in words and to use words effectively, whether orally or in writing. The foundation of this intelligence is laid before birth, when the fetus develops hearing while still in the womb. It continues to develop after birth. Authors, poets, newscasters, journalists, public speakers, and playwrights are people who exhibit high degrees of linguistic intelligence.

People who are strongly linguistic like to read, write, tell stories or jokes, and play word games. They enjoy listening to stories or to people talking. They may have a good vocabulary or a good memory for names, places, dates, and trivia. They may spell words accurately and communicate to others effectively. They might also exhibit the ability to learn other languages.

Verbal-linguistic intelligence can be stimulated and developed in the classroom by providing a language rich environment. Classrooms in every subject area should include activities to help students develop a passion for language through speaking, hearing, reading, and examining words. Have students write stories, poems, jokes, letters, or journals. Provide opportunities for impromptu speaking, rapping, debate, storytelling, oral reading, silent reading, choral reading, and oral presentations. Involve students in class discussions and encourage them to ask questions and listen. Invite students to use storyboards, tape recorders, and word processors. Plan field trips to libraries, newspapers, or bookstores. Supply nontraditional materials such as comics and crossword puzzles to interest reluctant students.

Writing, listening, reading, and speaking effectively are key skills. The development of these four parts of linguistic intelligence can have a significant effect on a student's success in learning all subject areas and throughout life.

Logical-Mathematical Intelligence

Logical-mathematical intelligence consists of:

- the ability to use numbers effectively
- the ability to use inductive and deductive reasoning
- the ability to recognize abstract patterns

This intelligence encompasses three broad, interrelated fields: math, science, and logic. It begins when young children confront the physical objects of the world and ends with the understanding of abstract ideas. Throughout this process, a person develops a capacity to discern logical or numerical patterns and to handle long chains of reasoning. Scientists, mathematicians, computer programmers, bankers, accountants, and lawyers exhibit high degrees of logical-mathematical intelligence.

People with well-developed logical-mathematical intelligence like to find patterns and relationships among objects or numbers. They enjoy playing strategy games such as chess or checkers, solving riddles, and logical puzzles or brain teasers. They organize or categorize things and ask questions about how things work. These people easily solve math problems quickly in their heads. They may have a good sense of cause and effect and think on a more abstract or conceptual level.

Logical-mathematical intelligence can be stimulated and developed in the classroom by providing an environment in which students frequently experiment, classify, categorize, and analyze. Have students notice and work with numbers across the curriculum. Provide activities that focus on outlining, analogies, deciphering codes, or finding patterns and relationships.

Most adults use logical-mathematical intelligence in their daily lives to calculate household budgets, to make decisions, and to solve problems. Most professions depend in some way on this intelligence because it encompasses many kinds of thinking. The development of logical-mathematical intelligence benefits all aspects of life.

Bodily-Kinesthetic Intelligence

Bodily-kinesthetic intelligence consists of:

- the ability to control one's body movements to express ideas and feelings
- the capacity to handle objects skillfully, including the use of both fine and gross motor movements
- the ability to learn by movement, interaction, and participation

Bodily-kinesthetic intelligence begins with the control of automatic and voluntary movement and progresses to using the body in highly differentiated ways. The skillful manipulation of one's body or an object requires an acute sense of timing and direction, as well as the ability to transform an intention into action. Examples of people who possess bodily-kinesthetic intelligence are a dancer using his or her body as an object for expressive purposes and a basketball player who manipulates a ball with finesse. This intelligence can be seen in inventors, mechanics, actors, surgeons, swimmers, and artists.

People who are strongly bodily-kinesthetic enjoy working with their hands, have good coordination, and handle tools skillfully. They enjoy taking things apart and putting them back together. They prefer to manipulate objects to solve problems. They move, twitch, tap, or fidget while seated for a long time. They cleverly mimic other's gestures.

Many people find it difficult to understand and retain information that is taught only through their visual and auditory modes. They must manipulate or experience what they learn in order to understand and remember information. Bodily-kinesthetic individuals learn through doing and through multi-sensory experiences.

Bodily-kinesthetic intelligence can be stimulated and developed in the classroom through activities that involve physical movements such as role-playing, drama, mime, charades, dance, sports, and exercise. Have your students put on plays, puppet shows, or dance performances. Provide opportunities for students to manipulate and touch objects through activities such as painting, clay modeling, or building. Plan field trips to the theater, art museum, ballet, craft shows, and parks.

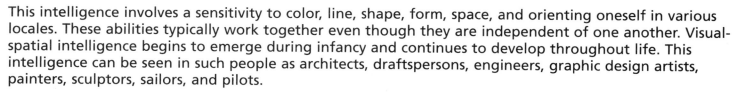

Visual-Spatial Intelligence

Visual-spatial intelligence consists of:

- the ability to perceive the visual-spatial world accurately
- the ability to think in pictures or visual imagery
- the ability to graphically represent visual or spatial ideas
- the ability to orient the body in space

This intelligence involves a sensitivity to color, line, shape, form, space, and orienting oneself in various locales. These abilities typically work together even though they are independent of one another. Visual-spatial intelligence begins to emerge during infancy and continues to develop throughout life. This intelligence can be seen in such people as architects, draftspersons, engineers, graphic design artists, painters, sculptors, sailors, and pilots.

Spatially skilled people enjoy art activities, jigsaw or visual perception puzzles, and mazes. They like to construct three-dimensional models. These people get more out of pictures than words in reading materials. They may excel at reading maps, charts, and diagrams. Also, they may have a good sense of direction.

Visual-spatial intelligence can be stimulated and developed in the classroom by providing a visually rich environment in which students frequently focus on images, pictures, and color. Provide opportunities for reading maps and charts, drawing diagrams and illustrations, constructing models, painting, coloring, and solving puzzles. Play games that require visual memory or spatial acuity. Use guided imagery, pretending, or active imagination exercises to have students solve problems. Use videos, slides, posters, charts, diagrams, telescopes, or color-coded material to teach the content area. Visit art museums, historical buildings, or planetariums.

Visual-spatial intelligence is an object-based intelligence. It functions in the concrete world, the world of objects and their locations. This intelligence underlies all human activity.

Musical Intelligence

Musical intelligence consists of:

- a sensitivity to pitch (melody), rhythm, and timbre (tone)
- an appreciation of musical expressiveness
- an ability to express oneself through music, rhythm, or dance

Dr. Gardner asserts that of all forms of intelligence, the consciousness-altering effect of musical intelligence is probably the greatest because of the impact of music on the state of the brain. He suggests that any normal individual who has had frequent exposure to music can manipulate pitch, rhythm, and timbre to participate with some skill in composing, singing, or playing instruments. The early childhood years appear to be the most crucial period for musical growth. This intelligence can be seen in composers, conductors, instrumentalists, singers, and dancers.

Musically skilled people may remember the melodies of songs. They may have a good singing voice and tap rhythmically on a surface. Also, they may unconsciously hum to themselves and may be able to identify when musical notes are off-key. They enjoy singing songs, listening to music, playing an instrument, or attending musical performances.

Musical intelligence can be stimulated and developed in the classroom by providing opportunities to listen to musical recordings, to create and play musical instruments, or to sing and dance. Let students express their feelings or thoughts through using musical instruments, songs, or jingles. Play background music while the students are working. Plan field trips to the symphony, a recording studio, a musical, or an opera.

There are strong connections between music and emotions. By having music in the classroom, a positive emotional environment conducive to learning can be created. Lay the foundations of musical intelligence in your classroom by using music throughout the school day.

Interpersonal Intelligence

Interpersonal intelligence consists of:

- the ability to focus outward to other individuals
- the ability to sense other people's moods, temperaments, motivations, and intentions
- the ability to communicate, cooperate, and collaborate with others

In the early form of this intelligence, a young child possesses the ability to discriminate among the individuals around him or her and to detect their various moods. In the more advanced form of this intelligence, one can read the intentions and desires of other individuals and act upon that knowledge. This intelligence includes the ability to form and maintain relationships and to assume various roles within groups. The competence is prominent in political and religious leaders, salespeople, teachers, counselors, social workers, and therapists.

Interpersonally skilled people have the capacity to influence their peers and often excel at group work, team efforts, and collaborative projects. They enjoy social interaction and are sensitive to the feelings and moods of others. They tend to take leadership roles in activities with friends and often belong to clubs and other organizations.

Interpersonal intelligence can be developed and strengthened through maintaining a warm, accepting, supporting classroom environment. Provide opportunities for students to collaboratively work in groups. Have students peer teach and contribute to group discussions. Involve the students in situations where they have to be active listeners, be aware of other's feelings, motives, and opinions, and show empathy.

The positive development of interpersonal intelligence is an important step toward leading a successful and fulfilling life. Interpersonal intelligence is called upon in our daily lives as we interact with others in our communities, environments, nations, and world.

Intrapersonal Intelligence

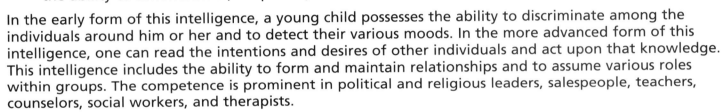

Intrapersonal intelligence consists of:

- the ability to look inward to examine one's own thoughts and feelings
- the ability to control one's thoughts and emotions and consciously work with them
- the ability to express one's inner life
- the drive toward self-actualization

This intelligence focuses on the ability to develop a complete model of oneself, including one's desires, goals, anxieties, strengths, and limitations, and also to draw upon that model as a means of understanding and guiding one's behavior. In its basic form, it is the ability to distinguish a feeling of pleasure from one of pain, and to make a determination to either continue or withdraw from a situation based on this feeling. In the more advanced form of this intelligence, one has the ability to detect and to symbolize complex and highly differentiated sets of feelings. Some individuals with strong intrapersonal intelligence are philosophers, spiritual counselors, psychiatrists, and wise elders.

Intrapersonally skilled people are aware of their range of emotions and have a realistic sense of their strengths and weaknesses. They prefer to work independently and often have their own style of living and learning. They are able to accurately express their feelings and have a good sense of self-direction. They possess high self-confidence.

Intrapersonal intelligence can be developed through maintaining a warm, caring, nurturing environment that promotes self-esteem. Offer activities that require independent learning and imagination. During the school day, provide students with quiet time and private places to work and reflect. Provide long-term, meaningful learning projects that allow students to explore their interests and abilities. Encourage students to maintain portfolios and examine and make sense of their work. Involve students in activities that require them to explore their values, beliefs, and feelings.

Intrapersonal intelligence requires a lifetime of living and learning to inwardly know, be, and accept oneself. The classroom is a place where teachers can help students begin this journey of self-knowledge. Developing intrapersonal intelligence has far-reaching effects, since self-knowledge underlies success and fulfillment in life.

Naturalist Intelligence

Naturalist intelligence consists of:

- the ability to understand, appreciate, and enjoy the natural world
- the ability to observe, understand, and organize patterns in the natural environment
- the ability to nurture plants and animals

This intelligence focuses on the ability to recognize and classify the many different organic and inorganic species. Paleontologists, forest rangers, horticulturists, zoologists, and meteorologists exhibit naturalist intelligence.

People who exhibit strength in the naturalist intelligence are very much at home in nature. They enjoy being outdoors, camping, and hiking, as well as studying and learning about animals and plants. They can easily classify and identify various species.

Naturalist intelligence can be developed and strengthened through activities that involve hands-on labs, creating classroom habitats, caring for plants and animals, and classifying and discriminating species. Encourage your students to collect and classify seashells, insects, rocks, or other natural phenomena. Visit a museum of natural history, a university life sciences department, or nature center.

Naturalist intelligence enhances our lives. The more we know about the natural world, and the more we are able to recognize patterns in our environment, the better perspective we have on our role in natural cycles and our place in the universe.

REFERENCES

Armstrong, Thomas. *Multiple Intelligences in the Classroom*. Alexandria, VA: Assoc. for Supervision and Curriculum Development, 1994. A good overview of the Multiple Intelligences Theory and how to explore, introduce, and develop lessons on this theory.

Campbell, Linda, Bruce Campbell, and Dee Dickerson. *Teaching and Learning Through Multiple Intelligences*. Needham Heights, MA: Allyn and Bacon, 1996. An overview and resource of teaching strategies in musical, spatial, bodily-kinesthetic, interpersonal, and intrapersonal intelligences.

Gardner, Howard. *Frames of Mind: The Theory of Multiple Intelligences*. New York: Basic Books, 1993. A detailed analysis and explanation of the Multiple Intelligences Theory.

————. *Multiple Intelligences: The Theory in Practice*. New York: Basic Books, 1993. This book provides a coherent picture of what Gardner and his colleagues have learned about the educational applications of the Multiple Intelligences Theory over the last decade. It provides an overview of the theory and examines its implications for assessment and teaching from preschool to college admissions.

Haggerty, Brian A. *Nurturing Intelligences: A Guide to Multiple Intelligences Theory and Teaching*. Menlo Park, CA: Innovative Learning, Addison-Wesley, 1995. Principles, practical suggestions, and examples for applying the Multiple Intelligences Theory in the classroom. Exercises, problems, and puzzles introduce each of the seven intelligences.

Lazear, David. *Seven Pathways of Learning: Teaching Students and Parents About Multiple Intelligences*. Tucson: Zephyr Press, 1994. Assists in strengthening the child's personal intelligence and in integrating multiple intelligences into everyday life. Includes reproducibles and activities to involve parents.

————. *Seven Ways of Knowing: Teaching for Multiple Intelligences*. Arlington Heights, IL: IRI/SkyLight Training and Pub, 1992. A survey of the theory of multiple intelligences with many general activities for awakening and developing the intelligences.

Verbal-Linguistic Intelligence

Word Play

Understanding a language involves more than just literal interpretation of the words heard or read. It also involves understanding *idioms*—common expressions that have meanings beyond that of the words that make them up. Some common idioms are listed below. Encourage students to add others. Then invite them to create a class dictionary or word wall of idioms that includes humorous illustrations of the literal meanings.

all thumbs	backseat driver
blow up	burn the candle at both ends
catch cold	cut corners
go to the dogs	hang in there
hit the ceiling	keep your chin up
put your foot in your mouth	play by ear

Book Panels

Invite four or five students who have read the same book to participate in a panel discussion. Explain that a panel discussion is an opportunity for a group to present different views about a topic. Give panel members time to prepare short answers to questions such as those listed below.

- What do you think was most interesting about the book?
- What did the book teach you about life or about yourself?
- Who was your favorite character and why?
- What is your opinion of the author's writing style?
- If you were to change something about the book, what would it be?

For the discussion, seat panel members facing the rest of the class—their audience. You can serve as panel moderator, or have a student take that part, asking each participant to respond to a question in turn. You may also want to open up the discussion to additional questions from the classroom audience.

It's All in How You Say It

Engage the class in a short discussion about which they consider more important: *what* someone says—or *how* they say it. Then write the following sentence on the chalkboard or on chart paper: *He is my best friend.* Point to the word *he* and ask a volunteer to read the sentence aloud, stressing that word. Discuss how the emphasis determines the meaning of the sentence. (He is my best friend, as opposed to someone else.) Then have a volunteer read the sentence a second time, with the emphasis on the word *is.* Continue, with a different word stressed in each reading. Discuss how the meaning of the sentence changes as the word being emphasized does.

Logical-Mathematical Intelligence

Sentence Building

Review common parts of speech: nouns, pronouns, verbs and linking verbs, adverbs, adjectives, articles, and prepositions. Then invite students to practice writing sentences using different patterns, or combinations, of these parts of speech. For example, ask students to create a sentence with a noun-verb-noun pattern, such as *Tim saw Keesha.* Other patterns are listed below.

noun-verb	Mother called.
noun-verb-adverb	Children grow quickly.
article-noun-verb-preposition-noun	The principal ran to school.
adjective-noun-verb-adverb	Colorful leaves blow lightly.

noun	verb	noun
Tim	saw	Keesha

It's Just Not Logical

Admit to students that sometimes English just doesn't make sense! How can we give someone a "definite maybe"? The two words have opposite meanings. And what about calling something "pretty ugly"? Can it really be both?

Explain that such expressions are called *oxymorons*—phrases that are made up of terms that are contradictory in meaning. Introduce students to some of the oxymorons listed below. For each expression, ask students to identify what is illogical about the pairing.

almost perfect	taped live	bad health
freezer burn	genuine imitation	good grief!
larger half	least favorite	war games
mild interest	modern history	nondairy creamer
old news	only choice	rock opera

Visual-Spatial Intelligence

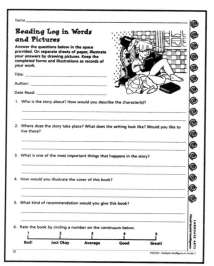

page 18

Reading Portfolios

Ask students to keep portfolios that depict their reading progress for a set period of time. Use pocket folders or have students make portfolios by folding 11-by-18-inch construction paper in half to make 11-by-9-inch folders. Offer students several copies of the **Reading Log in Words and Pictures** worksheet provided on page 18. Have them complete a log entry for each book they read during the collection period.

At the end of the specified period of time, ask students to select at least one of the books they read and respond to it creatively. Students can choose one of the projects below or use their own ideas.

· Make a poster that advertises the book.

· Design a new book jacket.

· Create illustrations for the story.

· Make a story-based mobile.

· Create a three-dimensional model of a scene from the story.

Comic-Strip Book Reports

Display an assortment of comic strips from the Sunday newspaper. Provide time for students to read and enjoy the comics. Then discuss how the creators of these strips use comics as storytelling vehicles. Be sure students understand that stories progress sequentially from frame to frame; that dialogue is usually shown in balloons; and that the illustrations depict most of the plot's action.

Encourage students to retell favorite books in comic-strip format. Their comic strips can retell an entire story or a selected chapter. Students will need to outline the major happenings in the book or chapter before determining how to show the action in comic strip form and what dialogue they want to add. Provide time for students to share their finished work.

LANGUAGE ARTS

Bodily-Kinesthetic Intelligence

Mime Time

Introduce the word *pantomime.* Explain that the word comes from the Greek word *mime,* which means the act of portraying a character or situation through bodily movement.

Provide time for students to practice simple pantomiming exercises. Assign a student an activity from those listed below and ask him or her to communicate the idea through bodily movement only. Classmates should try to identify the activity being pantomimed.

milking a cow	putting on winter boots and mittens
setting a table	making a bed
playing baseball	putting on ice skates and skating

Speaking in Signs

Expose children to a different kind of language—the manual alphabet used by many hearing-impaired individuals. You may be able to find a volunteer who can demonstrate this language to students. (Check in the yellow pages under Social and Human Services.) Or locate a chart of the manual alphabet in books such as *The Macmillan Visual Desk Reference* (Macmillan, 1993) or *A Show of Hands,* by Mary Beth Sullivan (Addison-Wesley, 1985). Teach children how to form the letters of the alphabet. Then practice finger spelling words.

Extend this activity by teaching signs that represent whole words. Point out that spoken language is based on an alphabet, just as sign language is. But alphabet letters are combined to form words that are spoken as single units, not spelled out letter by letter. Sign language works much the same way. Signs are combined and adapted to form whole words and phrases. Some simple examples to teach are the following:

Idea

Idea	Sign I at the forehead, then move hand away from face.
Elevator	Sign E about chest high and move hand up.
King	Sign K at the right shoulder; move diagonally across body.
Water	Form a W and tap it on the chin.

Musical Intelligence

A Chorus of Voices

Introduce the word *chorus* and ask a volunteer to define it. Help students realize that a presentation by a chorus doesn't necessarily have to be sung. The word describes something done in unison by a group, such as a chorus line of dancers, or a group speaking in one voice. Ask students to consider what choral presentations have in common, helping them to see that understanding rhythm and tempo are important to any kind of activity done in unison.

Invite students to do a choral reading in two parts. Explain that it is important to practice so the words sound musical—spoken in unison with a pleasing rhythm and tempo. Begin by dividing a poem such as "The Little Turtle," by Vachel Lindsay (*Sing a Song of Popcorn,* Scholastic, 1988), into speaking parts by alternating every line. Or choose a reading from *Joyful Noise: Poems for Two Voices,* by Paul Fleishman (HarperCollins, 1988).

The Music of Poetry

Write the following nursery rhyme on the chalkboard:

Humpty Dumpty sat on a wall.

Humpty Dumpty had a great fall.

All the king's horses and all the king's men

Couldn't put Humpty together again.

Ask students to read the rhyme in unison. Discuss the fact that, like a song, a poem has rhythm. Have students analyze the rhythm by counting the syllables in each line. They should note that the rhyming lines have the same number of syllables, and emphasized—or accented—syllables fall in the same place.

Next ask students to study the pattern of the rhyme. They will notice that line 1 rhymes with line 2 and line 3 rhymes with line 4. Explain that rhyming patterns are sometimes shown by letters of the alphabet. The pattern for this rhyme is A-A-B-B.

Give students copies of the **Rhythm and Rhyme** worksheet found on page 19. Invite them to have fun writing rhymes to fit different patterns.

page 19

Interpersonal Intelligence

Reader Interviews

Invite students to interview one another about books they have read. First discuss the kinds of interview questions that might elicit the most interesting answers. Write sample questions on chart paper for students to reference. Help students understand that they want to avoid questions that can be answered with a simple "yes" or "no." Then provide time for each student to write three or four general questions. Arrange the class in pairs, trying to match students who have not read one another's book choices. Have them take turns interviewing one another. When the interviews are complete, provide time for each interviewer to introduce the person interviewed, give the title of the book the person read, and explain whether or not the answers to the interview questions made the interviewer want to read the book being discussed.

Storytelling in the Round

Explain to students that a group of mystery writers in Florida decided to have fun writing a book together, called *Naked Came the Manatee* (Hiaasen et al, Putnam, 1977). They did so by each writing a chapter. But they didn't plan out the whole story first. They just kept passing the chapters along from person to person. Each writer had to keep the story going according to what was already written.

Invite students to have fun trying their own group storytelling. Have them sit in a circle. Choose a student to begin the story, or provide the class with a one- or two- sentence story starter. Then have them continue the story, each adding a few sentences in turn. Stress that they must listen carefully to each storyteller so they can add something that makes sense. Students toward the end of the circle need to be sure their contributions begin to wind up the action or solve some of the problems that have arisen. You may want to tape-record the students' work so later they can listen to the story as a whole.

Book Versus Video

After sharing a read-aloud book with the class, present a video based on the book. Then divide the class into small groups to discuss the book and the video. Have them consider topics such as which format they liked best and why, whether the storyline differed from one format to another, if characters looked and sounded as students had imagined them, and so on. At the end of the discussion, ask groups to take a vote about which format of the story was most popular. Compile and tabulate the votes. The list below suggests appropriate books that have been produced in video form.

- *Abel's Island* by William Steig (Farrar, Straus, Giroux, 1976)
- *The Best Christmas Pageant Ever* by Barbara Robinson (HarperCollins, 1972)
- *Charlie and the Chocolate Factory* by Roald Dahl (Puffin, 1964) Video title is *Willy Wonka and the Chocolate Factory*
- *The Hundred Penny Box* by Sharon B. Mathis (Puffin, 1986)
- *Charlotte's Web,* by E. B. White (Harper & Row, 1980)
- *The Mouse and the Motorcycle,* by Beverly Cleary (Dell, 1965)
- *Follow the Drinking Gourd,* by Jeanette Winter (Knopf, 1988)
- *The Paper Bag Princess,* by Robert Munsch (Annick-Press, 1980)
- *Jumanji,* by Chris Van Allsburg (Houghton Mifflin, 1981)
- *The Phantom Tollbooth,* by Jules Feiffer (Knopf, 1961)
- *Sarah, Plain and Tall,* by Patricia MacLachlan (HarperCollins, 1985)
- *Skylark,* by Patricia MacLachan (Houghton Mifflin, 1995)

Intrapersonal Intelligence

Life's Frights

Have students listen with closed eyes as you read aloud Maya Angelou's poem, "Life Doesn't Frighten Me" (Steward, Tabori, and Chang, 1993). Ask them to reflect on the images the poet's words bring to mind. After reading, provide time for students to express their reactions to the poem orally or in writing.

Then share the picture book version of the poem, illustrated by Jean-Michel Basquiat. Invite students to consider whether the artist's images match their own mental pictures. Have them reflect upon the mood of the illustrations and how well they think the art conveys the meaning of the poem. Invite students to write and illustrate their own poems about coping with the frightening things in life.

A Personal Viewpoint

Review with students the difference between first- and third-person writing using appropriate examples from their classroom reading. Next have them

choose a passage from a book or story written in the third person. Encourage students to think about what the main character would know and feel about the situation being described. Then ask them to rewrite the selected passage in the first person, explaining what happened from the viewpoint of the character and describing what he or she thought, felt, and learned.

Naturalist Intelligence

page 20

Sharp Senses

To give your students an opportunity to "stop and smell the roses" and put the experience into words, offer your them copies of the **Sharp Senses** worksheet found on page 20. As a homework assignment, have them choose a spot outdoors for observation and record what they see, hear, touch, smell, and taste. (Point out that many observation opportunities will not involve taste, and that section may be blank.) Have students keep their completed forms and ask them to refer to them during the class's next creative writing exercise.

Nature Word Flowers

A simple flower drawing can serve as a tool for expanding your students' vocabulary while increasing their awareness of nature. Choose a topic related to the natural world and write it in a flower shape. Then add stem and leaf lines to the flower for words related to that topic. The example at right is based on the theme "Nature Sounds." Students added the words *whoosh, screech, plunk, rumble, giggle* to describe the sound the nouns on the left make. Keep the completed flower, and other word flowers created by the class, on display so they can be referred to during reading and writing time.

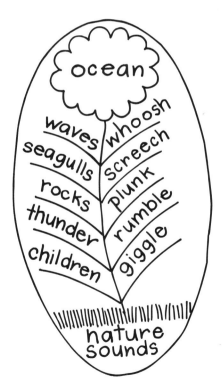

Reading Log in Words and Pictures

Answer the questions below in the space provided. On separate sheets of paper, illustrate your answers by drawing pictures. Keep the completed forms and illustrations as records of your work.

Title: _____

Author: _____

Date Read: _____

1. Who is the story about? How would you describe the character(s)?

   _____

   _____

2. Where does the story take place? What does the setting look like? Would you like to live there?

   _____

   _____

3. What is one of the most important things that happens in the story?

   _____

   _____

4. How would you illustrate the cover of this book?

   _____

   _____

5. What kind of recommendation would you give this book?

   _____

   _____

6. Rate the book by circling a number on the continuum below.

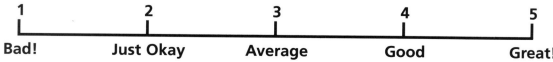

1	2	3	4	5
Bad!	Just Okay	Average	Good	Great!

LANGUAGE ARTS
Visual-Spatial Intelligence

Rhythm and Rhyme

Have fun writing short rhymes with different rhyming patterns. Be sure your poems have a pleasing rhythm. You can accomplish this by making sure rhyming lines have a similar number of syllables and are accented in the same way.

Write a rhyme for each of the patterns below.
Remember that lines that have the same letter of the alphabet must rhyme.

Pattern   Poem

A   _____

B   _____

A   _____

B   _____

Pattern   Poem

A   _____

A   _____

B   _____

B   _____

Pattern   Poem

A   _____

B   _____

C   _____

A   _____

B   _____

C   _____

Pattern   Poem

A   _____

A   _____

B   _____

B   _____

A   _____

LANGUAGE ARTS
Musical Intelligence

Sharp Senses

Successful writers are good observers of nature. They use their senses as they react personally to experiences in the natural world. How does the snow sound underfoot? What does a warm summer rain smell like? How does the surface of a flower petal feel? A writer might use these observations later when describing something in a story.

Go for a walk or sit quietly in a natural setting and observe. Then record everything your senses tell you about the experience. Write your observations in colorful detail so you will remember them. Don't just record that you heard the sound of a waterfall. Instead, describe the sound. Was the water rushing, trickling, or dripping? Later, use some of the observations in your own writing.

My observation experience: _____

Sights: _____

_____

_____

Sounds: _____

_____

_____

Textures: _____

_____

_____

Smells: _____

_____

_____

Tastes: _____

_____

_____

LANGUAGE ARTS
Naturalist Intelligence

Verbal-Linguistic Intelligence

Exploration Research

Provide students with copies of the **Exploring for Explorers** worksheet shown on page 28. Explain that the chart is missing some information. Their job is to work with a partner to consult reference materials and add as many of the missing facts as they can. Provide time to use the library or set up a classroom collection of materials to use for research. Include encyclopedias, electronic materials, social studies texts, biographical dictionaries, and so on.

Once pairs have completed as much of the chart as possible, go over the answers as a group. Ask volunteers to explain where they located missing information.

Then ask each student to choose one explorer to research in greater depth. Have them report to the class in oral or written form. Reports should include information about the life of the individual, the importance of the discovery, and the impact of the discovery on people who lived in the region at the time or on the world in general.

Exploring for Explorers

What do you know about explorers of the past? Explore the encyclopedia, a biographical dictionary, your social studies text, and other references to fill in the missing information on the chart below.

Year	Explorer	Accomplishment	Nationality
1488	Bartolomeu Dias	Sailed around Africa's Cape of Good Hope	1.
1492	2.	First European to reach the West Indies	Italian; explored for Spain
1497	John Cabot	First European to reach Newfoundland	3.
1498	4.	Discovered a sea route to India	Portuguese
1513	Vasco Núñez de Balboa	5.	Spanish
1513	6.	First European to discover Florida	Spanish
1519	Hernán Cortés	7.	Spanish
1533	8.	Conquered Peru for Spain	Spanish
	Hernando de Soto	First European to discover the Mississippi River	9.
1603	Samuel de Champlain	Explored the Saint Lawrence River	10.
1610	Henry Hudson	11.	English
1673	12.	First to navigate length of the Mississippi River	French
1767	James Cook	13.	English
1804	Meriwether Lewis and William Clark	14.	American
1805	Charles Fraser	Explored Canada west of the Rocky Mountains	15.
1819	16.	First to find the Northwest Passage in Arctic	English
1842	John Fremont	Explored America west of the Rocky Mountains	17.
1856	David Livingstone	18.	Scottish
1909	Robert Peary	19.	American
1911	20.	Led first expedition to reach South Pole	Norwegian

page 28

A Geography Dictionary

Invite students to create an illustrated dictionary of geography terms. Write the terms you want students to learn on individual index cards. Place these and an assortment of reference materials in a social studies learning center. Include a dictionary, an atlas, and library books about geographic concepts. Encourage interested students to choose a card and define and illustrate the term. Completed cards can be filed alphabetically in a card box and used as references. Some terms you may want to include are listed below:

altitude	environment	nomad
archipelago	erosion	plateau
fjord	prime meridian	arid
globe	rain forest	axis
gulf	relief map	hemisphere
revolution	boundary	inlet
rotation	canyon	island
scale of miles	cartographer	isthmus

sea level	climate	jet stream
timberline	compass rose	latitude
sphere	continental shelf	longitude
topography	culture	meridian
delta	desert	natural resources

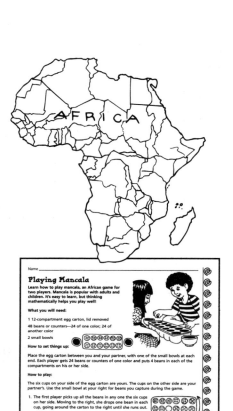

page 29

Logical-Mathematical Intelligence

Mancala

Have students locate Africa on the globe. Then explain that they are going to learn a game that is popular in many African countries. The game is known by different names in different countries, but is most commonly called mancala. Have children choose partners and provide each pair with a copy of the **Playing Mancala** worksheet found on page 29. (To make the game, each pair will need to bring a cardboard egg carton from home.)

Make a Story Map

Invite students to create illustrated maps of scenes or settings of favorite stories. As much as possible, maps should be based on information contained in the story. For example, a map of Zuckerman's farm from *Charlotte's Web,* by E.B. White (Harper and Row, 1980), should contain the barn, farmhouse, fenced fields, feeding troughs, road, and trees mentioned in the story. Each map should include details such as a key, a distance scale, and a compass rose.

Terrific Time Lines

Invite students to create a large time line based on some aspect of the social studies curriculum. For example, you may want them to create a time line of inventions, exploration, settlement of the United States, the Civil Rights movement, or another pertinent topic. Once the topic is determined, work with students to complete the time line as follows:

1. Identify the starting and ending dates for the time line.

2. Determine how to best subdivide the time line—into 1, 10, 20, or 100 year periods, for example.

3. Measure the space available—a classroom or hallway wall, sheet of mural paper, large bulletin board, top of the chalkboard, etc.

4. Compute the amount of space that can be allotted to each time period and label the time line.

5. Assign small groups or individuals to specific time spans. Have them research appropriate facts to be included on the time line. Each item to be included should be labeled and illustrated on the time line itself, or on an index card that can be attached to the time line.

Bodily-Kinesthetic Intelligence

Relief Maps

Display a large relief map for students to study. Ask them to consult the map key to see how different elevations are shown. Have them identify areas of high and low altitude and features such as lakes and rivers. Discuss how such features might have influenced settlement of the area. Then invite students to make their own three-dimensional relief maps, using the home-made clay recipe at right. The map should be put on a base of heavy cardboard or thin plywood. You may want to specify certain features to be included: mountains, a river and delta, plateau, area below sea level, and so on. Each batch makes enough dough for one good-sized map, so you may want to ask a number of parent volunteers to each make one or more batches. When the maps are completely dry, the dough can be painted with tempera paint.

Demonstrating History

Invite students to demonstrate a craft or activity from the past. Presenters should introduce their demonstrations by explaining when the craft or activity began and when it was popular, who might have engaged in it, whether or not it is still done, and so on. Suggestions include demonstrations such as the following:

Making a sampler	Drying apples or other fruit
Dancing a reel or another dance	Pressing flowers
Using Morse Code	Writing in Roman numerals

Everyday Clay

4 cups baking soda

2 cups cornstarch

2 1/2 cups water

Combine baking soda and cornstarch in a large saucepan. Add the water. Cook over medium heat, stirring constantly, until dough forms a ball. Let dough cool, then knead until smooth. Store in airtight container.

Visual-Spatial Intelligence

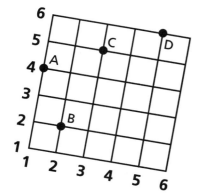

Where in the World?

Review the use of coordinates by making a simple grid on the chalkboard. Label the grid as shown at left. Have students practice identifying the location of each of the letters shown on the grid. For your reference, coordinates are listed below.

A (X4,Y1)   B (X2,Y2)

C (X5,Y3)   D (X6,Y5)

Then review the terms *latitude* (imaginary lines that measure distance north and south of the equator) and *longitude* (imaginary lines that measure distance east and west of the prime meridian.) Display a large map of the United States that shows lines of latitude and longitude. Help students use what they know about coordinates to locate large cities at the latitudes and longitudes listed below.

Latitude 40°, Longitude 75° (Philadelphia, PA)

Latitude 30°, Longitude 95° (Houston, TX)

Latitude 40°, Longitude 105° (Denver, CO)

Latitude 35°, Longitude 90° (Memphis, TN)

Latitude 35°, Longitude 85° (Chattanooga, TN)

Getting Oriented

Invite students to play a directional game based on "Simon Says." First locate and label North in the classroom. Then have students stand. Explain that you will be giving geographical directions. If a direction is preceded by the words, "Atlas says...," students are to turn and face that way. If the suggestion is not preceded by those words, students should ignore it. Begin with simple directions—east, west, etc. Then move on to intermediate directions—northwest, southeast, north-northeast, east-southeast, and so on.

Map Puzzles

Reproduce maps of geographical areas the class is studying, or use old maps. Invite students to create jigsaw puzzles from the maps. First maps should be glued to a stiff paper backing. When the glue is dry, maps can be cut into irregular pieces. Store each map puzzle in a separate plastic bag or manila envelope labeled with the city, country, or continent it features.

Musical Intelligence

Different Places, Different Sounds

Expose students to the diverse musical traditions of the world. There are many ways to build a collection of interesting music. Ask students to bring recordings of ethnic music from home, raid your own collection, and borrow from the school music teacher or public library. Try to include music that features instruments such as the following: African drum or balafon (a xylophone-like instrument), West Indian steel drum, Indian sitar, Japanese zither or lute, Ethiopian or Irish harp, Scottish bagpipe, Spanish guitar, and Appalachian dulcimer.

Each day devote time to a different selection. First identify the instrument or instruments featured and the country the music represents. Then have students listen and respond to the music verbally or in writing. Discuss how each selection is similar or dissimilar to the music of other countries.

Interpersonal Intelligence

Broadcast Time

Stage classroom news broadcasts. Have students work in small groups, each taking on a different role. Roles can include researchers, writers, editors, announcers, producers, newscaster, weather persons, sportscasters, and so on. Ask each group to plan and present a ten-minute broadcast set in current times or in an era being studied. The group should work together to identify stories to be featured in the newscast. Then they can divide up the tasks according to their roles. Researchers will gather material. Writers use this material to create short reports that answer the questions *who, what, when, where, how,* and *why.* Editors check each article for accuracy. Producers decide on the order of the broadcast, where the newscasters sit, and so on. Announcers introduce the news people. Provide time for each group to present its broadcast. You may want to videotape the broadcasts so students can view them later.

Who?
What?
When?
Where?
Why?
How?

Friendship Inventory

As students grow toward adolescence, peer relationships become increasingly important. Help students identify the qualities that lead to lasting friendship. Begin with a group discussion that analyzes the strengths and weakness of friendships described in a book the class has enjoyed. Appropriate titles include *How to Eat Fried Worms*, by Thomas Rockwell (Dell, 1973), *There's a Boy in the Girls' Bathroom,* by Louis Sachar, (Knopf, 1987), *Henry and Beezus,* by Beverly Cleary, (Avon, 1952), *Class President,* by Johanna Hurwitz (Morrow, 1990), and *The Hundred Dresses,* by Eleanor Estes (Harcourt, Brace, 1944).

Then offer students copies of the worksheet **Friendship Inventory** on page 30. Ask them to complete the inventory based on themselves or a character in one of the books mentioned above. Remind them that they are reflecting on friendship in general, not on specific people they know, so their responses shouldn't include names. After students have had time to complete the inventory, meet as a class or in small groups to discuss responses.

page 30

The Survival Game

Arrange students into groups of three and have members of each group count off from one to three. Ask them to imagine the following scenario:

You are hikers traveling together in a wilderness area and you have become lost. It is late autumn—the nights are cold, but there hasn't been any snow yet. The nearest town is at least a two-day walk, and there are no public roads until you reach that town. You are all wearing jeans, sweatshirts, heavy socks and hiking boots. In addition, each of you has the following:

Person 1	Person 2	Person 3
lighter	bag of raisins	jackknife
4-foot length of rope	ball of heavy twine	heavy wool blanket
compass	6 dried apples	pocket calculator
large plastic bag	mechanical pencil	several rubber bands

Have each group meet to discuss its survival plan. Using only what they have with them and what they can find in nature, how will they keep themselves warm, fed, and safe from predators? How will they find their way to safety? Then ask groups to share their plans with the rest of the class. Have them reflect on how they had to cooperate and whether any conflicts arose. Ask groups which items were most essential to their survival plan and whether any items were worthless to them.

Intrapersonal Intelligence

Goal Setting

At the beginning of a new unit of study, encourage students to set personal goals for their own learning. Discuss the kinds of goals they may want to consider: to learn something specific, to read three good books about the topic, to finish a project within the given time frame, to work cooperatively in a group, and so on. Have each student record his or her goal on a slip of paper. Then ask them to put the papers in a safe place. At the end of the unit, have students review their goals and reflect upon whether or not they were achieved. Encourage students to share their reflections in writing.

Keeping a Journal

Invite students to keep journals in which they write as a boy or girl of an era being studied. For example, if the class is studying the settlement of the United States, someone may choose to write journal entries as a child on the *Mayflower,* living in the Jamestown settlement, or traveling west on a covered wagon. Have them write a short entry every day during the course of the unit. Explain that journals should reflect what they have learned about everyday life in the era. However, they should also record the hopes, doubts, fears, and joys the person might have had.

Naturalist Intelligence

Earth Day

Read to your class *Earth Day,* by Linda Lowery (Carolrhoda, 1991), a short book about the history of Earth Day. Have your class research how Earth Day is observed in your community. Have students write reports on past Earth Days. Challenge them as individuals to change one habit in their lives that will help preserve the planet. Then challenge the class as a group to make a change that will benefit the natural world.

Nature at the Table

Have students research the plants and animals of the countries they are studying in social studies. Have them list which of these plants and animals provide food for the people of that country. Next ask the class to find meals that are prepared using these products. The class can be broken into groups, with each group assigned a different country, and each person within the group assigned a different dish. Have each group create a menu of breakfast, lunch, and dinner using the products of the country. Have students volunteer to bring some of the foods into class from home, or provide some yourself, and have an international food day.

Exploring for Explorers

What do you know about explorers of the past?
Explore the encyclopedia, a biographical dictionary,
your social studies text, and other references to fill in
the missing information on the chart below.

Year	Explorer	Accomplishment	Nationality
1488	Bartolomeu Dias	Sailed around Africa's Cape of Good Hope	1.
1492	2.	First European to reach the West Indies	Italian; explored for Spain
1497	John Cabot	First European to reach Newfoundland	3.
1498	4.	Discovered a sea route to India	Portuguese
1513	Vasco Núñez de Balboa	5.	Spanish
1513	6.	First European to discover Florida	Spanish
1519	Herman Cortés	7.	Spanish
1533	8.	Conquered Peru for Spain	Spanish
1541	Hernando de Soto	First European to discover the Mississippi River	9.
1603	Samuel de Champlain	Explored the Saint Lawrence River	10.
1610	Henry Hudson	11.	English
1673	12.	First to navigate length of the Mississippi River	French
1767	James Cook	13.	English
1804	Meriwether Lewis and William Clark	14.	American
1805	Charles Fraser	Explored Canada west of the Rocky Mountains	15.
1819	16.	First to find the Northwest Passage in Arctic	English
1842	John Fremont	Explored America west of the Rocky Mountains	17.
1856	David Livingstone	18.	Scottish
1909	Robert Peary	19.	American
1911	20.	Led first expedition to reach South Pole	Norwegian

Playing Mancala

Learn how to play mancala, an African game for two players. Mancala is popular with adults and children. It's easy to learn, but thinking mathematically helps you play well!

What you will need:

1 12-compartment egg carton, lid removed

48 beans or counters—24 of one color; 24 of another color

2 small bowls

How to set things up:

Place the egg carton between you and your partner, with one of the small bowls at each end. Each player gets 24 beans or counters of one color and puts 4 beans in each of the compartments on his or her side.

How to play:

The six cups on your side of the egg carton are yours. The cups on the other side are your partner's. Use the small bowl at your right for beans you capture during the game.

1. The first player picks up all the beans in any one the six cups on her side. Moving to the right, she drops one bean in each cup, going around the carton to the right until she runs out.

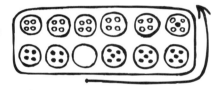

2. The second player picks up all the beans in one of his cups. Moving to the right, he drops one bean in each cup until he runs out.

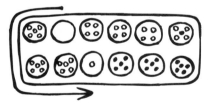

3. Take turns doing the same thing. If the last bean dropped by a player makes two or three beans in a cup on the opponent's side, the beans are "captured" and put into the player's small bowl. In addition, if the cup just before that one has only two or three beans, and is on the opponent's side, those beans are captured as well.

4. Keep going until one of you has no beans left on your side. You must pick up and drop a cupful of beans on each turn.

Mancala is easy, but it pays to think ahead. Try to figure out how to get two or three beans into one of the cups on your partner's side. And try not to leave any cups on your side with only one or two beans.

SOCIAL STUDIES Logical-Mathematical Intelligence

Friendship Inventory

Think about friendships you have or would like to have. How do you choose your friends? How do you make new friends? How do you and your friends treat one another? How important are friends to you? Once you've given some thought to those questions, finish the sentences below. Remember, there are no right or wrong answers. Be ready to discuss your thoughts with your classmates.

1. I like to be friends with people who are: _____

_____

2. A fun thing to do with a friend is: _____

_____

3. If a friend hurts my feelings, I: _____

_____

4. If I make a friend angry, I feel: _____

_____

5. I think friends should never: _____

_____

6. I think friends should always: _____

_____

7. I make friends by: _____

_____

8. One thing I'd change about my friendships is: _____

_____

9. One of my best memories about a friend is: _____

_____

10. When a friend moves away, I: _____

_____

11. Something I'll do with a friend in the future is: _____

_____

SOCIAL STUDIES
Interpersonal Intelligence

Verbal-Linguistic Intelligence

Math Stories

Invite students to write their own word problems. Explain that word problems tell a story. Within that story is enough information to solve the problem. Offer students the following example:

Theo, Ted, and Tran want to go to the movies. Tickets cost $5.25 each. Ted has $5.00, Theo has $2.00, and Tran has $7.50. How much more money do the boys need?

Ask students to analyze the story. First, have them identify the information they are given (how many boys need tickets, how much money each has, and how much one ticket costs). Then ask them to identify the problem being posed (how much more money is needed). And finally, ask students to determine how they would use the information given to solve the problem. Help students identify logical steps to find the answer.

Then invite students to write their own math stories in the form of word problems. They must be sure each problem states the question clearly and provides the information needed to find a solution. You may want to provide "story starters" such as buying a birthday gift, taking a trip, measuring for a rug, keeping scores or statistics at a sports event, and so on.

Prefixes: Mathematically Speaking

Knowing common math-related prefixes can help students understand the meanings of words. On the chalkboard, write each of the prefixes listed below.

(1) uni-   (2) du- or bi-   (3) tri-

(4) quad-   (5) quint-   (6) sex-

(7) sept-   (8) octa- or octo-   (10) dec-   (100) centi-

Invite students to use the meanings of the prefixes to help them answer questions you pose. Sample questions are listed below.

· How many babies are in a set of sextuplets? Quintuplets? Triplets?

· How many musical notes are in an octave?

· How many wheels are on a unicycle? A bicycle? A tricycle?

· In how many events would you compete in a decathalon? A triathalon? A biathalon?

· How many horns did triceratops have?

· How many years are in a century?

- How many legs does a quadruped have? A biped? An octopus?

- If a town is celebrating its centennial, how old is it?

- How many sides and angles are there in a triangle? A quadrilateral? An octagon? A decagon?

- If you're bilingual, how many languages do you speak? If you're trilingual?

- How many sets of three zeros are there in a billion?

- How many years are in a decade?

- How many decades has an octogenarian lived?

- How many centimeters are in a meter?

Note to the teacher: Students may ask about a prefix for the number nine. Explain that the prefix *non-* can mean nine. However, it usually means not. If students are interested, some examples of *non-* as a number prefix are: *nonagon* (figure with 9 sides and angles) and *nonet* (nine voices or instruments).

Logical-Mathematical Intelligence

Working in Order

Review the concept of order of operations with students. Write the following equation on the chalkboard: 6 + 3 x 2 = n. Ask a volunteer to solve the equation.

Then ask the student to explain the steps he or she took to solve the problem. Place parentheses to show the first operation the student completed. For example, if the student says, "First I added 6 and 3," you would draw parentheses around the first two numbers: (6 + 3) x 2 = 18.

Now rewrite the problem, placing the parentheses around the other pair of numbers, i.e., 6 + (3 x 2). Ask students to solve the equation again and compare their solution to the first one. What made the difference?

Point out that when working with equations that involve a combination of operations, the order of the operations matters. Operations grouped in parentheses should always be solved first. If necessary, use another equation as an example, grouping the numbers in two different ways.

$(12 \div 4) - (2 \times 1) = n$

$12 \div (4 - 2) \times 1 = n$

Offer each student a copy of the **Mystery Equations** worksheet found on page 40. Have them add parentheses to group the numbers in such a way

page 40

that each equation is correct.

Pascal's Triangle

Invite students to study Pascal's Triangle, a classic example of the patterns that can be found in math. Explain that Blaise Pascal lived in France in the seventeenth century. He was a man of many talents—author, thinker, scientist, and brilliant mathematician. In fact, Pascal is credited with making the first mechanical calculator. His device never really caught on. But Pascal is still so respected by mathematicians that one type of computer programming language bears his name.

One of Pascal's mathematical discoveries was a triangular arrangement of numbers. This arrangement is called Pascal's Triangle. The secret of the triangle is that each number is the sum of the two numbers just above it.

Offer students copies of the **Pascal's Triangle** worksheet, found on page 41. Point out that the pattern isn't complete, but there is enough information to discover what that pattern is. Have students work with partners to study the triangle and discover the pattern. Then ask them to fill in the missing numbers. Explain that they can extend the triangle if they wish—in fact they could go on and on and on, if they had the time and a large enough sheet of paper!

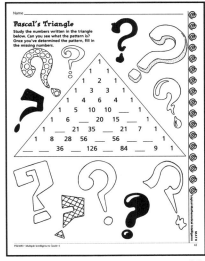

page 41

 # Bodily-Kinesthetic Intelligence

Body Angles

Give your class a quick review of angles, using arms instead of pencils. Ask students to stand far enough apart so they can stretch out their arms to the fullest. Then ask them to create a variety of angles using only one of their arms. For example, a right angle (90°) would be formed by holding the arm straight out from the shoulder and bent at the elbow with the hand pointing up. To form an obtuse angle (greater than 90°), the students would keep the upper arm steady and move the forearm down. To form an acute angle (less than 90°), they would move the forearm toward the shoulder. And a straight angle (180°) would be formed by stretching the arm straight out at shoulder height.

Measurable Moments

Ask students to think about how they might measure the length of an object without using standard tools of measurement. Help them understand that objects can be measured in non-standard units. As long as everyone understands what the unit being used is, the measurement is valid. You may want to share a humorous example of the use of non-standard measurements. In 1958 at the Massachusetts Institute of Technology, a student named Oliver Smoot was used to measure the length of a bridge. Oliver lay down repeatedly while friends kept track of how many body lengths it took to make it across the bridge. The MIT bridge is still labeled with that measurement: just over 364 "Smoots."

Invite students to use their own bodies as nonstandard units of measure. First decide what part of the body to use—you may want to have students use a finger or foot rather than the whole body. Then have them each measure something in the classroom or school environment. Ask students to share their results and discuss differences among the measurements. For example, 6 "Jasons" would be more than 6 "Eduardos" if Jason is a lot bigger than Eduardo.

Hopscotch Review

Lay out a hopscotch board using masking tape on the classroom floor or chalk on a paved area outside. Play the game by having students throw a marker or stone onto any space. They then follow the usual rules of hopscotch, hopping over that space on the way to the end and turning to make a return trip. Before picking up the marker or stone on the return trip, students must answer a review question based on the number in the square. For example, to review a family of multiplication facts, fill the squares with products and have the player supply a pair of factors that equal the number. To review fractions, write different fractions in each square. Then have players supply an equivalent fraction, a smaller fraction, a larger fraction, and so on.

Visual-Spatial Intelligence

Shapes and Designs

Display photographs or illustrations of patchwork quilts whose designs are made up entirely of geometric shapes. Have students identify circles, squares, triangles, trapezoids, rectangles, hexagons, and so on.

Then invite students to make paper quilt blocks that feature designs of their own creation. Explain that each design must include at least eight pieces and four different geometric shapes. The shapes can be different sizes and colors, but they must fit together to form one complete quilt square. Have students sketch out their designs first. Then they can measure to determine the size of each shape. Shapes can be cut from construction paper, colored paper, wallpaper samples, or wrapping paper. If the blocks are all the same dimension, a quilt can be assembled and hung on a wall for display.

"Seeing" Fractions

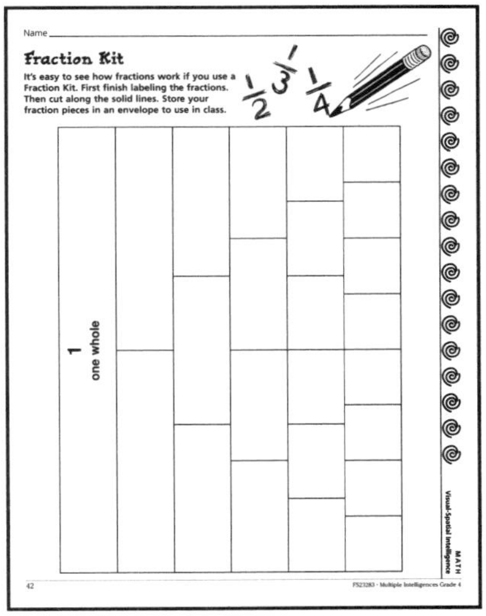

The complexities of fractions can be simplified by providing students with a helpful manipulative. Reproduce the **Fraction Kit** worksheet found on page 42, and offer each student a copy. Have students label each line of the diagram to show the fractional parts represented. Then ask them to cut carefully along the lines. Provide individual envelopes for storage of pieces.

Show students how to use the kits to answer questions about fractions. For each question, they should manipulate the pieces to show their answers. Encourage students to use the kits independently as they work with fractions. Sample questions are listed below:

- Which is larger: 1/2 or 2/3?
- What is another name for 1/2?
- How many eighths are in 1/2?
- Which is smaller: 3/4 or 7/8?
- How much is 1/2 + 1/3?
- What does 1/2 minus 1/4 equal?

Note: Students can also work in pairs, using two kits, to practice expressing improper fractions as mixed numbers.

Squares of Squares

Arrange children in pairs and give each pair 24 toothpicks. Ask them to arrange the toothpicks as shown at right. Then have partners count to determine the number of squares made by the toothpicks. If a pair counts nine squares, tell them to count again. Help them understand that any four small squares can be combined to make a large square. And the entire design makes an even larger square. (The answer is 14 different squares. The small squares in the middle columns are counted as part of more than one square. And the entire shape makes up a square.)

Provide each pair with 12 additional toothpicks and ask them to create an even larger square of squares. (The new square will have to be four toothpicks long on each side.) Then repeat the counting exercise.

Musical Intelligence

Math Rap

Information that is presented through the use of rhythm and rhyme is easier to remember. Invite students to create rap songs that will help them remember math concepts. Explain that a rap is like a song, with a definite pattern of rhythm and rhyme. However, the words are spoken, not sung. Teach the students the short rap at right and have them practice performing it. Then ask them to work individually or with a partner to create their own math

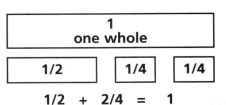

page 42

1 one whole

| 1/2 | | 1/4 | | 1/4 |

1/2 + 2/4 = 1

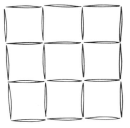

Geometry Rap

Nu-mer-a-tor

That's the name

For the number at the top

In the fraction game.

The one at the bottom

We learned a little later.

That number's called

The de-nom-i-na-tor.

raps. Have completed raps written on chart paper and displayed in the classroom.

Musical Fractions

Explain to students that when they read or write music, they are using fractions. Different types of notes stand for different lengths of sound. The names of the notes tell how they relate to one another in length.

On the chalkboard, write each of the notes shown below. Ask students if they can identify the notes. Then label each note with its name (shown in parentheses after the note itself).

Point out that the name of a note tells how long it is. In the same time it takes to play or sing one whole note, a musician can play or sing two half notes, four quarter notes, and so on.

On the board, write groupings of notes such as those shown, separated by vertical lines. For each grouping, have volunteers write the whole number or fraction that shows the relative length of the note. Help students realize that the sum of the fractions within each group is equal to one. (For your reference, fractions are written under the notes here.)

Choose several groupings and ask students to try tapping them out, being sure the half notes are only half as long as the whole notes, and so on. You may also want one of your student musicians to demonstrate different types of notes being played on a flute, recorder, classroom piano, or another instrument.

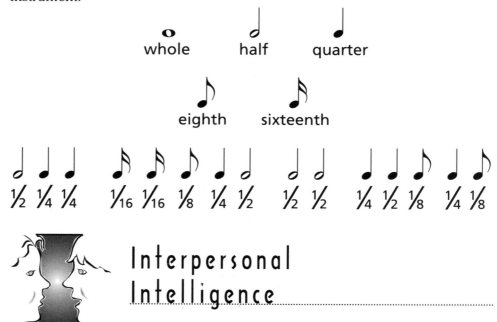

Riddle Math

Write some or all of the following riddles on the chalkboard or chart paper. Arrange students in groups of three or four. Ask groups to work together to solve the riddles. However, they must do more than agree upon a solution. Each group must also provide an explanation of the thinking they used to solve the riddle. Set a time limit for the groups, allowing approximately three minutes per riddle. Possible thought processes that could be used are included in parentheses below. However, students may have other ideas. Accept any explanation that is logical.

1. A girl was walking to school when she saw a boy walking toward her, pulling a wagon. There were six kittens in the wagon. Each kitten had ten fleas. How many were going to school? (Only one. The boy, the kittens, and the fleas were all headed the other way.)

2. You have two United States coins that equal thirty cents. One of them is not a nickel. What coins do you have? (A quarter and a nickel. The quarter is the "one" coin that is not a nickel.)

3. How much dirt would you have in a hole that is 2 feet wide, 2 feet long, and 3 feet deep? (None. A hole doesn't have anything in it.)

4. A boy saw some ducks swimming across the pond. One duck was in front of two ducks. One duck was behind two ducks. And one duck was between two ducks. How many ducks did the boy see? (There were three ducks. The first one had two ducks behind it, the second one was in between the other two, and the third one had two ducks ahead of it.)

5. There are 12 pennies in a dozen. How many dimes are in a dozen? (12. A dozen means twelve of something. A dozen dimes is worth more than a dozen pennies, but you still have 12!)

Peer Tutors

Post a Peer Tutor Chart where students can sign up to work with classmates in certain areas of math. Some students may be comfortable offering to help a classmate with fractions, decimals, long division, or another area of the math curriculum. But every student should be encouraged to sign up as a tutor, even if only to assist a classmate with practicing multiplication and division flash cards. When students want help, they can go to the chart to locate a tutor who could assist them during free time.

Intrapersonal Intelligence

Letters of Explanation

After learning a multistep mathematical process such as multiplication by two numbers or reducing fractions to their lowest common terms, ask students to write instructions about the process. Their instructions should be written as if they were explaining the process to a student who had been absent for the lesson. Collect the letters and save them. Later, when reviewing the process, hand the letters back. Ask students to review by rereading what they wrote. Have them reflect upon how accurately their original letters outlined the process. Invite them to revise their letters if they wish.

Setting Goals

Encourage students to set personal goals for learning multiplication and division facts. For example, if the class has regular timed tests on facts, goals can center on increasing the number of facts answered accurately. Or a student might set a goal of increasing the number of flash cards that can be solved correctly in a set amount of time.

Naturalist Intelligence

Nature's Geometry Scavenger Hunt

Arrange students into pairs or small groups and send them on a Nature's Geometry Scavenger Hunt. Students should search for some of the shapes, angles, and lines listed below in natural items such as the fork of tree branches, flowers, rocks, leaves, etc. Set the boundaries of the search area according to your circumstances, for example, the outside play area, a cross-country track, or a field trip site (or have them do the activity as homework at a natural site of their choosing). Vary your list according to terms taught.

Explain that groups must stay together as they search. They should check off each item found and note where the item was spotted. These records must be specific. Set a time limit for the search. When the time is up, gather the groups together and see how many items were found by each group. Spot-check accuracy by asking each group to share what they wrote about several of its finds. If some of the items on the list can't be found, discuss where one might find them in nature.

Search for...

circle	right angle	cylinder
acute angle	horizontal line	rectangle
obtuse angle	vertical line	hexagon
semicircle	octagon	oval
cone	triangle	set of parallel lines
set of perpendicular lines		

Weather Patterns

Have students keep track of the weather over a period of at least three weeks. Collect data about precipitation, extent and type of cloud cover, high and low temperatures, and wind speed and direction. Data can be a combination of observation, measurement, and use of published or broadcast weather reports. Keep track of the information on a class-sized weather chart.

At the end of the time period, have students study the data they collected to see if there are any patterns revealed. Did the air temperature seem to be affected by precipitation or the amount of cloud cover? Were specific cloud formations associated with specific weather phenomenon? Did wind direction appear to have anything to do with precipitation? Discuss the students' observations.

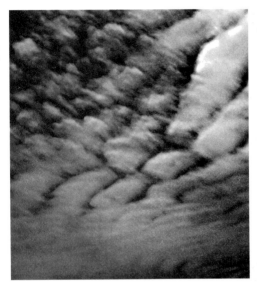

Mystery Equations

The equations below are all missing something important. The numbers aren't grouped! Add parenthesis to show how to group numbers to get the correct answer. Check your work by writing the completed equation on the line at the right.

Example: 400 ÷ 10 + 10 = 50

Answer: (400 ÷ 10) + 10 = 50   40 + 10 = 50 _____

1. 24 ÷ 3 − 1 = 7   _____

2. 65 − 2 x 6 = 53   _____

3. 400 ÷ 8 x 5 = 10   _____

4. 103 + 23 − 100 = 26   _____

5. 6 x 2 + 4 = 36   _____

6. 22 + 101 x 0 = 0   _____

7. 42 ÷ 7 + 21 ÷ 3 = 13   _____

8. 6 x 0 + 12 x 3 = 36   _____

9. 4 + 4 + 6 x 6 = 44   _____

10. 6 ÷ 3 + 6 − 3 + 6 + 3 = 14   _____

11. 100 ÷ 10 x 50 ÷ 10 = 50   _____

12. 3 x 4 + 5 + 6 + 8 − 7 = 24   _____

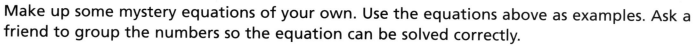

Make up some mystery equations of your own. Use the equations above as examples. Ask a friend to group the numbers so the equation can be solved correctly.

a. _____

b. _____

c. _____

Logical-Mathematical Intelligence   M A T H

Pascal's Triangle

Study the numbers written in the triangle below. Can you see what the pattern is? Once you've determined the pattern, fill in the missing numbers.

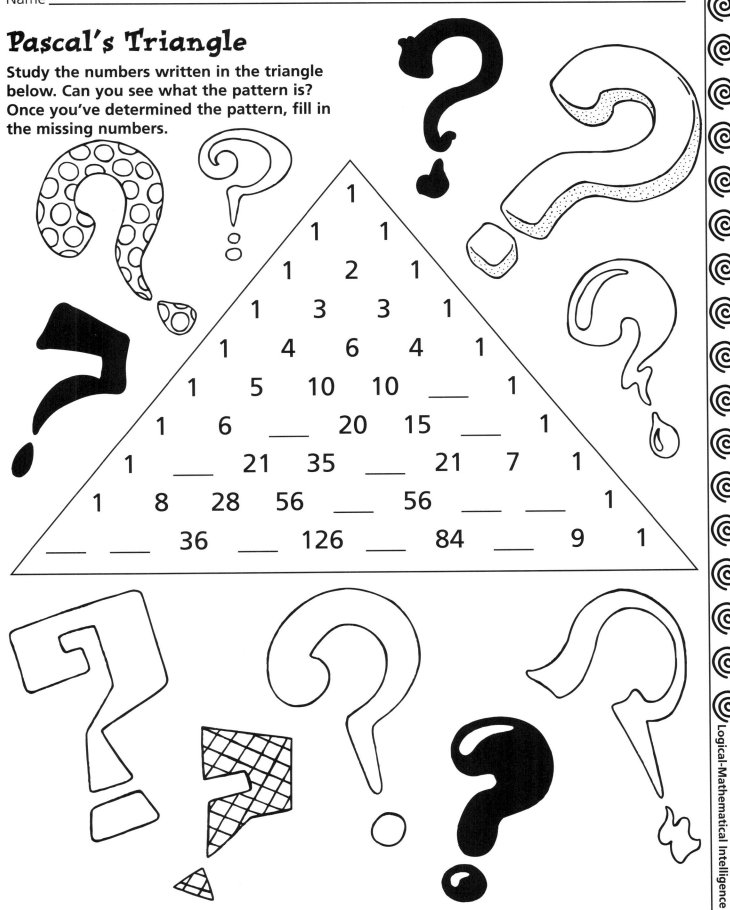

```
                    1
                 1     1
               1    2    1
            1    3    3    1
          1    4    6    4    1
        1    5   10   10   __   1
      1    6   __   20   15   __   1
    1   __   21   35   __   21   7   1
  1    8   28   56   __   56   __   __   1
__   36   __  126   __   84   __   9   1
```

MATH

Logical-Mathematical Intelligence

Fraction Kit

It's easy to see how fractions work if you use a
Fraction Kit. First finish labeling the fractions.
Then cut along the solid lines. Store your
fraction pieces in an envelope to use in class.

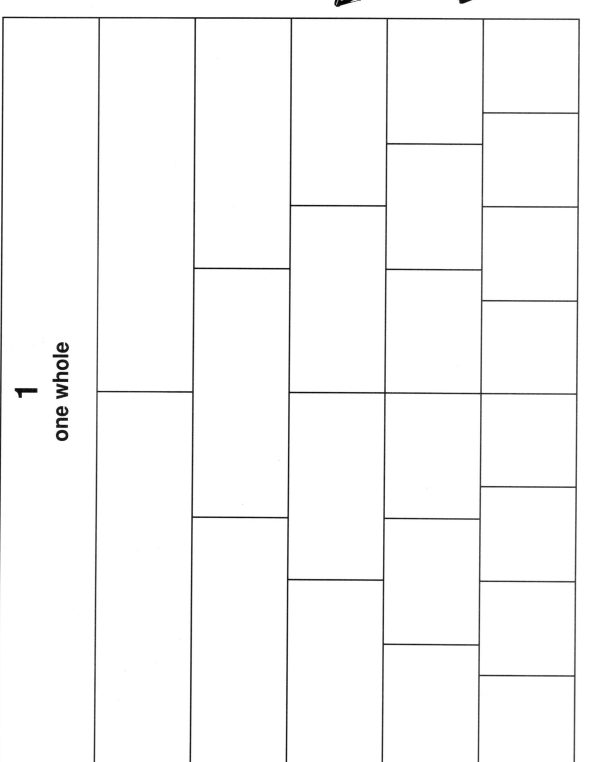

1
one whole

Verbal-Linguistic Intelligence

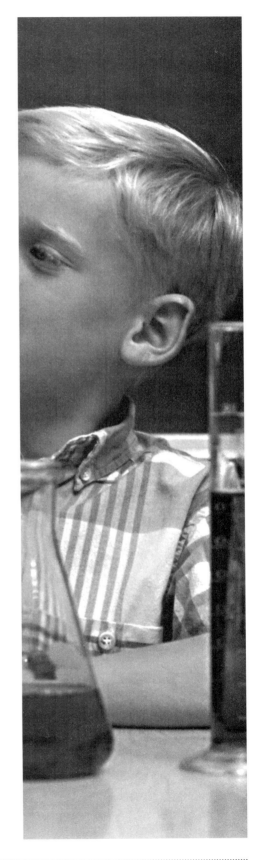

Science Heroes

Set up a display of biographies and autobiographies of scientists. Encourage students to select one scientist they would like to learn more about. Ask students to share what they learn about the scientist in the form of a poster. The poster should give the scientist's name, scientific specialty, nationality, and birth date. It should also list a few facts about the person's life and a summary of scientific achievements. Display the posters in the classroom as a Gallery of Science Heroes.

Some appropriate titles are listed below. Consult with your community or school librarian to find others.

- *Black Pioneers of Science and Invention,* by Louis Haber (Harcourt Brace, 1993)
- *The First Woman Doctor,* by Rachel Baker, a biography of Elizabeth Blackwell (Scholastic, 1987)
- *Marie Curie,* by Louis Sabin (Troll, 1985)
- *My Life With the Chimpanzees,* by Jane Goodall (PB Publishing, 1988)
- *Leonardo da Vinci,* by Norman F. Marshall (Silver Burdett, 1980)
- *Rachel Carson: Pioneer of Ecology,* by Kathleen Kudlinski (Puffin, 1989)
- *Thomas Alva Edison,* by Louis Sabin (Troll, 1983)
- *The Wright Brothers at Kitty Hawk,* by Donald J. Sobol (Scholastic, 1987)

Science Analogies

Review the use of analogies with students. Write the following example on the chalkboard: A tennis ball goes with a racket in the same way that a baseball goes with a _____. Ask students if they can fill in the missing word (bat). Discuss how they determined the answer. Help them understand that to solve the problem they need to identify the relationship of the first two terms (a tennis ball is used with or hit by a racket) and then think of a word that goes with baseball in the same way.

Show students how the sentence below would be written as an analogy:

tennis ball : racket as baseball : bat

Point out that identifying the relationships within an analogy means knowing something about the terms being used. Explain that they can use what they know about science to solve the following analogy:

liquid : water as oxygen : _____

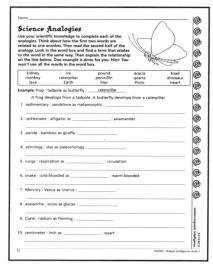

page 52

Ask them to identify the relationship between the first two words. (Water is an example of a liquid.) Then have them identify the missing word and explain how the relationship between the first two words helped them determine the answer. (What is oxygen an example of? A gas.) Provide students with copies of the **Science Analogies** worksheet found on page 52. Have them complete the analogies and explain their thinking in determining the answers.

It's Greek!

Point out that sciences that are very different still have something in common. Write the terms *geology, astrology, biology, and paleontology* on the chalkboard. Ask students to identify a similarity between the terms. If they have trouble, prompt them to take a look at the spelling of the words. All end with the suffix *-logy*. Explain that this suffix comes from Greek and means *the science of*.

Ask students to use the dictionary and other references to identify the branch of science being described by each of the following *-logies*. You may want to assign one or two words to each student, or have them work in groups. For your reference, answers are included in parentheses.

astrology (stars)

biology (life, living things)

cardiology (heart)

cosmology (universe)

cytology (cells)

ecology (environment)

entomology (insects)

geology (earth, rocks)

herpetology (reptiles, amphibians)

hydrology (water)

neurology (nervous system)

ornithology (birds)

otology (ear)

paleontology (fossils, ancient life)

pathology (disease)

seismology (earthquakes)

toxicology (poisons)

zoology (animals)

Logical-Mathematical Intelligence

Drawing to Scale

Explain to students that scientists are concerned with accuracy. When making observations, they want their notes to reflect things as they actually are. So they often draw things "to scale." This means that a smaller measurement is substituted for a larger one. For example, when drawing a tree, a scientist might use a scale of 1/4 inch to 10 feet. A tree that is 40 feet high in real life would be 1 inch high in the scale drawing.

Offer students sheets of graph paper to use when practicing drawing to scale. Have them decide on a scale that will work. If drawing small objects, such as leaves, the scale might be 1 square is equal to 1 inch. For larger objects, such as trees, the scale might be 1 square is equal to 12 feet. Encourage students to add captions and labels to their drawings as well. Display the completed scale drawings in the classroom.

Time to Experiment

Discuss with students the steps in the scientific process. A simple explanation of the process is at right.

Discuss the idea that responsible scientists rely on the scientific method. Their hypotheses aren't always correct, but any experiment gives a scientist additional factual information to use when developing a new hypothesis.

Invite students to practice using the scientific method themselves as they design and carry out experiments. Remind them that a well-designed experiment uses a "control." A control is a parallel experiment that is exactly the same except for one factor. For example, an experiment to see how sunlight affects a bean plant would use two identical plants. They would be treated exactly the same way except for the amount of sunlight they receive.

Offer students copies of the **Experiment Time** worksheet provided on page 53. Ask them to record information about their experiments on the worksheet. As they conduct their experiments, they should record observations and conclusions on the form as well. The list below suggests some problems students may want to investigate.

- Does an object's shape affect its ability to float?
- Does the surface on which a ball rolls affect its speed?
- Does distance affect the speed at which an object drops?
- Does water weigh more in its frozen state than in its liquid state?
- What kind of soil absorbs the most water?

1. **Identify a problem or question.**

2. **Formulate a hypothesis: a logical guess based on the known facts.**

3. **Design an experiment to test the hypothesis.**

4. **Carry out the experiment, observing and recording the results.**

5. **Draw conclusions based on the results of the experiments.**

page 53

Bodily-Kinesthetic Intelligence

Life-Size Systems

Have students create life-size charts of the body systems. Ask them to work in pairs to outline each other's body on mural paper or brown wrapping paper. Then have each student choose one of the body systems to diagram on his or her outline: circulatory, respiratory, nervous, digestive, reproductive, or muscular. Provide a variety of print and electronic reference materials for students' use and remind them to make their diagrams as realistic as possible.

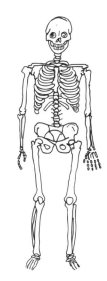

When the diagrams are completed, ask students to cut along the edges of the body outlines. Post the shapes on the classroom wall and have students take turns presenting the different body systems, using their outlines as visual references.

Animal Family Upset

Invite students to play Animal Family Upset, a scientific version of the classroom game Fruit Basket Upset. First record characteristics of animal families the class has studied on slips of paper, such as mammals, birds, reptiles, amphibians, fish, and insects. Place these in a box or paper bag. Then assign each student the name of one of the animal families.

To play, have students sit in their own seats. Choose one student as the leader. The leader pulls out a slip of paper and reads the characteristic, for example: *Always has wings*. Students designated as members of the bird family get up and move to an empty seat. At the same time, the leader tries to get to an empty seat. The student left standing becomes the new leader.

The list below features some animal family characteristics you might use as clues when playing the game.

Always has wings (bird)	Warm-blooded (mammal and bird)
Can have wings (bird, insect)	Breathes with gills (fish, amphibian)
Three body parts (insect)	Scaly skin (fish, reptile)
Has antennae (insect)	Cold-blooded (fish, reptile, amphibian, insect)
Has six legs (insect)	Has no legs (fish, reptile [snake])
Doesn't lay eggs (mammal)	Covered with fur or hair (mammal)
Has feathers (bird)	Needs air (all animals)

Going Afield

Provide students with the opportunity to experience science first-hand. Plan a field trip that relates to a science topic being studied. Some suggestions for field trip destinations are listed below. There may be other possibilities within your community.

- natural history museum
- seashore, lakeshore, or riverbank
- science center
- park or forest preserve
- planetarium
- botanical park or arboretum
- observatory

- commercial greenhouse
- zoo or zoological park
- meteorology station
- nature or wildlife preserve
- university physics, chemistry, or biology lab
- aquarium
- landfill or recycling center

Before the trip, identify concepts that students may see in action. Discuss these ideas with the class. Have students take notepads with them on the trip and encourage them to record their observations throughout the field trip, especially in terms of the concepts identified. Provide time to share these observations when the class returns to school.

Visual-Spatial Intelligence

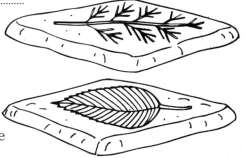

Impressions of Nature

Take students on a nature walk around the school grounds or to a nearby park. Have them collect natural objects with interesting shapes and textures—fallen leaves, evergreen twigs with needles, pine cones, sticks, pieces of rough bark, stones, and so on. Remind them that items should be on the ground, not removed from a living tree or bush.

In the classroom, offer each student a ball of modeling clay that will air-dry. Have them form the clay into a square tile about 1/2 inch thick. Then show them how to carefully press an object into the clay to create an impression. Once the impression is made, the object should be removed and the clay should be set aside to dry.

Food Webs

Review with students the concept of a food chain—the sequence within which a larger animal eats a smaller one, all the way down to plant-eaters. Then discuss food webs—the interaction of different food chains. Offer students copies of the **Food Web** worksheet found on page 54. Have them read and follow the directions to complete the activity.

Roll an Insect

Have fun reviewing the body parts of an insect. Teach students a paper-and-pencil version of the popular game Cootie. Students can play in groups of two to six. Each group will need one die and pencil and paper for every

page 54

group member. As in Cootie, the object of the game is to be the first to complete an entire insect. But in this version, the insect is drawn—and it represents a real creature. Students roll the die to determine what body part they can draw on each turn. Their insect is completed when they have drawn a creature with head, thorax, abdomen, six legs, and two antennae. (Since not every insect has wings, they can be drawn when the rest of the insect is completed.) Assign numbers on the die and body parts according to the chart below:

If player throws a:	1	2	3	4	5	6 (wild throw)
He/she can draw:	head	thorax	abdomen	leg	antenna	any part

Musical Intelligence

Setting Nature to Music

Invite students to listen to and enjoy classical music with nature themes. Identify the name and composer of the piece. Then play a short selection from the larger work. Provide time for students to give their reactions, asking them to consider how the composer used music to represent nature. Were there passages that sounded like water or waves? Like wind or rain? Some appropriate compositions include:

- *La Mer,* by Claude Debussy
- *The Four Seasons,* by Antonio Vivaldi
- *Grand Canyon Suite,* by Ferde Grofé
- *The Water Music* by George F. Handel

The Sound of Music

Review the concept that without vibration there is no sound. Ask students to think of musical instruments that are familiar to them and how each uses vibration to create its sound. When a guitar string is plucked, it vibrates. When you blow into a flute, the air vibrates. When a tambourine is shaken, all its parts vibrate. In each case, these vibrations travel through the air in the form of sound waves. The pitch, or frequency of a sound, depends on how long the sound waves are. The faster an object vibrates, the shorter the wavelength of the sound it makes. The shorter the wavelength, the higher the pitch is.

Invite students to experiment with sound and pitch by making simple "junk" instruments such as the following:

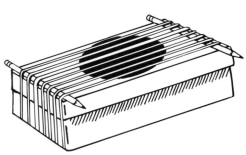

Shoe-box Strings: Cut an oval hole in the center of the lid of a shoe box. Replace the lid. Then stretch 7 rubber bands of different thicknesses around the shoe box the long way. Arrange the rubber bands from thinnest to

thickest. Slide a pencil under the rubber bands at either end of the shoe box. Pluck on the strings to create sound. How does the pitch change as you move from the thickest to the thinnest string?

Bottle Woodwind: Make a row of seven glass bottles that are approximately the same size and shape. Pour a small amount of water into the first bottle. Then add water to the other bottles with each one having more water than the one before it. Create sound by blowing across the tops of the bottles. How does the pitch change as you move from the emptiest to the fullest bottle?

Junk Percussion: Make several sets of claves from sticks of varying thicknesses. For each set of claves, the two sticks should be about the same thickness. Try striking each set in turn, beginning with the thinnest. How does the pitch change from set to set?

 # Interpersonal Intelligence

Science Clubs

Invite interested students to start a science club. The club can focus on science in general, or on a specific topic such as ecology, chemistry, nature, geology, and so on. Arrange supervision so students can meet during recess time, a free class period, or a before- or after-school activity time. At the first meeting, have club members name the club, decide how often they want to meet, and determine what kind of activities they will have at meetings. They may also want to create membership cards and posters that give information about meeting times and activities. Examples of activities for club meetings are listed at right.

- **Invite someone to speak on a science topic.**
- **Visit a junior high or high school science lab.**
- **Plan and carry out experiments.**
- **Organize a classroom or school-wide science fair.**
- **View a video on a science topic.**

Class Recycling Center

Have students work together to organize a classroom recycling center. Provide containers labeled for the different kinds of recyclables accepted in your area. Students can create a flyer that encourages others in the school building to bring their clean, dry, recyclable material to the recycling center. As material is collected, have students observe and discuss concepts such as the following:

- What code numbers are found on the majority of the plastics being turned in?
- What kind of material takes up the most space per pound?
- How many pounds of recyclables can the class collect within a specific time frame?
- How many cubic feet of landfill space would it take to accommodate one week's worth of recycling?

Plan to end the activity with a field trip to the local recycling center to turn in the materials collected.

Intrapersonal Intelligence

Invention Magic

Discuss with students how inventions have improved life. Have them imagine how their lives would be different if things they take for granted had never been invented—the automobile, the television, and the electric light bulb, for example. Then ask them to think about other inventions that may not be so obvious, but make life far better for people. For example, vaccines keep children from dying of diseases that once killed many.

Encourage students to come up with their own ideas for inventions that would make life easier or better for themselves or for someone else. Explain that their ideas can be as far-fetched as they want. Inventions can be in the fields of transportation, entertainment, industry, food production, education, medicine—any aspect of their lives. Have them describe and illustrate their inventions, explaining exactly how each is intended to improve life.

Reflections on the Natural World

The beauty and wonder of the natural world have always inspired creativity. Set up a learning center where students can reflect upon examples of this creativity and make their own responses to nature. Include a selection of picture books that depict nature themes in a poetic fashion; writing materials; and art materials such as paper, scissors, colored pencils, paints, markers, and old magazines. Invite students to read a selection independently and reflect upon how the author uses words and illustrations to express his or her feelings about the subject. Then encourage students to use the materials to create their own artistic responses to the same theme. Responses can include stories, poetry, abstract or realistic paintings, drawings, and collages. Some appropriate books to include are:

- *Birches,* by Robert Frost (Henry Holt, 1988)
- *How the Forest Grew,* by William Jasperson (Morrow, 1992)
- *Catskill Eagle,* by Thomas Locker (Putnam, 1991)
- *Mojave,* by Diane Siebert (HarperCollins, 1992)
- *The Desert Is Theirs,* by Byrd Baylor (Simon and Schuster, 1975)
- *A River Ran Wild,* by Lynne Cherry (Houghton Mifflin, 1995)
- *The Great Kapok Tree*, by Lynne Cherry (Harcourt, Brace, Jovanovich, 1990)

Make Animal Tracks

Ask each student to choose an animal and research what its tracks look like. Don't forget animals such as dinosaurs, snakes, and those that drag their tail. Students should note that front tracks of animals are often different than hind tracks. A good reference for tracks is *Secrets of a Wildlife Watcher,* by Jim Arnosky (Beech Tree, 1991). Have students make tracks on long pieces of paper.

Track stamps can be made with a raw potato. Draw the track on the potato half and cut away the excess potato until the track protrudes about a quarter inch. This can be inked and used as a stamp.

Each student should label his or her track. The finished products can be attached to each other and hung in the classroom for display. Drawings of leaves, rocks, flowers, etc., can be added to the track mural to make it more lifelike and decorative.

Bird Watching

Develop students' naturalist intelligence by having the class observe birds throughout the school year. Have the class build several different types of bird feeders. If possible, place these feeders in a place where they can be viewed from a window in the classroom. On a regular basis, have the students observe the kinds of birds that visit each feeder. Have students keep a journal of the names of the birds, which feeder the birds visited, and when they were observed (time and day). If the students don't know the bird's name, have them draw and color a picture of the bird. Then provide reference books for the students to make graphs showing how frequently a particular bird was observed.

Name ______________________________

Science Analogies

Use your scientific knowledge to complete each of the analogies. Think about how the first two words are related to one another. Then read the second half of the analogy. Look in the word box and find a term that relates to the word in the same way. Then explain the relationship on the line below. One example is done for you. Hint: You won't use all the words in the word box.

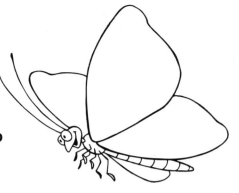

kidney	ice	pound	acacia	toad
monkey	caterpillar	penicillin	quartz	dinosaur
lava	Earth	liter	Pluto	heart

Example: frog : tadpole as butterfly : caterpillar

A frog develops from a tadpole. A butterfly develops from a caterpillar.

1. sedimentary : sandstone as metamorphic : ______________

____

2. rattlesnake : alligator as ______________ : salamander

____

3. panda : bamboo as giraffe : ______________

____

4. astrology : star as paleontology : ______________

____

5. lungs : respiration as ______________ : circulation

____

6. snake : cold-blooded as ______________ : warm-blooded

____

7. Mercury : Venus as Uranus : ______________

____

8. avalanche : snow as glacier : ______________

____

9. Curie : radium as Fleming : ______________

____

10. centimeter : inch as ______________ : quart

____

SCIENCE
Verbal-Linguistic Intelligence

Experiment Time

Use the form below to identify a problem, record a hypothesis, plan an experiment to test your hypothesis, record your observations, and come to some conclusions about how accurate your hypothesis was.

Problem or question:

_____

_____

Hypothesis: _____

_____

_____

Experiment Plan: _____

_____

_____

Materials Needed: _____

_____

_____

Procedure: _____

_____

_____

Observations: _____

_____

_____

Conclusions: _____

_____

_____

SCIENCE Logical-Mathematical Intelligence

Food Web

How do people fit into the food chain? Study the plants and animals shown below. Then draw lines and arrows to create a food web that shows the relationships among them. Arrows should point toward the plant or animal being eaten. More than one arrow can be included for each element of the food web. An example is drawn for you.

In the space below use words or illustrations to create another example of a food web. Include different plants and animals than those shown above.

SCIENCE

Visual-Spatial Intelligence

Verbal-Linguistic Intelligence

Storybook Dramas

Encourage students to work in small groups to select classic tales or contemporary picture books to dramatize for younger children. Once a group has made its selection, the members should plan how they want to present the story to their audience. Suggestions include a puppet show, an oral retelling of the story in parts, a short play, or a choral reading based on the story. Provide time for groups to create scripts and any props or costumes they want to use. After allowing time for practice, have students visit younger classes to make their presentations.

Fine Arts Vocabulary

Create a classroom chart of fine arts vocabulary words. Head each column of the chart with a different area of the arts: *Drama; Dance; Music; Visual Arts.* Provide an assortment of reference materials, blank index cards, and tape. As students encounter new words, have them record each on an index card, add a simple definition, and tape the cards in place on the chart in the appropriate columns.

Insights Into Opera

Use picture books to introduce opera to your students. *Behind the Golden Curtain: Hansel and Gretel at the Great Opera House,* by E. Lee Spruyt, (Four Winds, 1986) takes students on a tour of New York City's Metropolitan Opera House as preparations are made for a presentation of Humperdink's opera, *Hansel and Gretel. The Magic of Mozart,* by Ellen Switzer, (Atheneum, 1994) features a wealth of information about the composer's life and work, as well as a section about his opera *The Magic Flute.* Photographs of a Salzburg marionette performance of the opera (Harcourt, Brace, 1997) illustrate the book. Told by Leontyne Price, *Aïda* is a richly illustrated retelling of the story behind the great Verdi opera of the same name.

Logical-Mathematical Intelligence

Puzzling Dimensions

Artist M.C. Escher once said, "I often seem to have more in common with

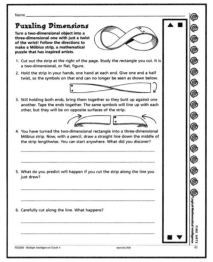

page 61

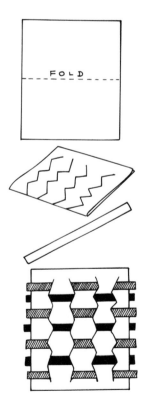

mathematicians that with my fellow artists." This comment is easy to understand when studying the artist's work. Expose students to a particularly interesting mathematical concept that Escher turned into art—the Möbius strip. (If possible, show students a print of the artist's woodcut Möbius Strip II [Red Ants].) Explain that the Möbius strip is named for a nineteenth-century German mathematician, August Möbius. Möbius was a pioneer in the field of topology, which deals with the properties of geometric figures on a surface. The Möbius strip starts out as a two-dimensional rectangular strip. But when one end of the strip is rotated 180° and the ends are then joined together, it becomes a three-dimensional figure with what seems to be one continuous surface.

Offer students copies of the **Puzzling Dimensions** worksheet found on page 61. Invite them to follow the directions and explore this interesting multi-dimensional puzzle.

Paper Weaving

Students are probably familiar with the concept of paper weaving, in which strips of paper are woven in and out of slits cut in a larger background piece. Encourage them to follow the steps at left as they experiment with this art form to create interesting irregular patterns. Display the finished weavings where students can see the interesting patterns created.

1. Fold a sheet of 8 1/2-x-11-inch or 11-x-18-inch colored paper in half vertically.

2. Create a "loom" by cutting jagged or wavy slits from the fold to a point approximately 1 inch from the open edge.

3. From a contrasting color or colors of paper, cut strips equal to or slightly longer than the width of the loom. Strips can all be the same width, or this measurement can vary.

4. Weave the strips in and out of the slits on the loom. Trim the edges if necessary.

Bodily-Kinesthetic Intelligence

Grown-up Finger Painting

Finger painting isn't just for little kids. Invite students to experiment with the feel of paint as they create a work of art with finger paints. Have them cover sheets of finger paint paper with paint. Then let them experiment with creating patterns in the wet paint using their hands, combs, feathers, small twigs, and other objects. Students should wear old clothes or art smocks for this activity.

Demonstrating an Art

Invite interested students to demonstrate the arts to their classmates through performances that highlight their own skills. These skills might include ballet, tap, or interpretative dance; playing a musical instrument; singing; presenting a dramatic reading from a play; and so on. Before each performance, the artist should explain what he or she will be demonstrating, how the skill was learned, and other information that might interest the members of the audience or help them better understand the demonstration.

Visual-Spatial Intelligence

Classic Comparisons

Provide students with visual references of well-known works of art to use for comparison purposes. Suggested points of comparison and artists whose works might be used are:

- Use of light and shadow: Vermeer, da Vinci, Titan, Rembrandt
- Shape and form: Cézanne, van Gogh, Picasso, Mondrian
- Use of color: Monet, van Gogh

Ask students to study at least two different works and discuss the similarities and differences between them. You may also want students to determine which artist's style they prefer and why.

Musical Intelligence

Listening to Instruments

Invite students to listen to a recording of Prokofiev's *Peter and the Wolf* as they study various musical instruments and the sounds they make. The words to the story are spoken with musical accompaniment, making the piece accessible to young listeners. And the instruments used to represent various characters are easy to pick out. A flute captures the twittering of a bird. The slinking of the cat is depicted by a clarinet. The low, sad sound of the oboe is the duck, and Peter's grandfather speaks in the grumbling tones of the bassoon. Challenge students to name the instruments that represent each character.

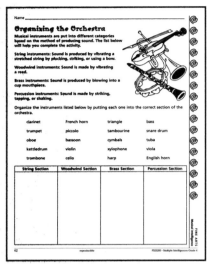

page 62

Instrument Families

Provide students with copies of the **Organizing the Orchestra** worksheet found on page 62. Make reference materials available as they complete the worksheets.

Round and Round

Have students sing "Row, Row, Row Your Boat," "Frère Jaques," or "Kookaburra" in unison. Then have them sing the same song as a round—with the class divided into four groups. Each group begins singing one line later than the group ahead of it.

Discuss with students the different sound created when the song is sung as a round. Then play a recording of a fugue by Johann Sebastian Bach. Explain that a fugue uses the same technique—a recurring melody sung at different times. Ask students to listen to Bach's music to study and enjoy the repeated melodies.

Interpersonal Intelligence

Collaborative Murals

Invite students to work together to create group murals using various media. The subject of the murals can be related to a curriculum topic or can be the choice of the group. Provide each group with a 4- to 5-foot sheet of mural paper, white freezer paper, or brown wrapping paper. Have groups plan out their murals first, discussing how the topic will be depicted, what elements will be shown, how they will be placed, and what will be the responsibility of each member in actually creating the mural. Encourage groups to consider using mixed media—paints, markers, colored pencils, pastels, cut-paper, and collage materials—as they create their collaborative murals.

Drama in the Classroom

Encourage interested students to work in groups and present short plays to their classmates. Presentations can be as simple as a dramatic reading of the parts. Students can also stage their plays as full-scale productions with costumes, sets, and props. Check your school and community library for published plays. The library may also subscribe to *Plays: The Drama Magazine for Young People*. The magazine is published monthly from October through May. Each issue contains scripts suitable for middle and lower grade students. Skits and puppet shows are also featured. For subscription membership, contact Plays, Inc., 120 Boylston Street, Boston, MA 02116-4615.

Intrapersonal Intelligence

Getting Into a Role

Ask students to keep logs of television shows they watch for a period of two or three days. As they watch, they should take notes about the different emotions being expressed and how the actors communicate these emotions to the audience.

At the end of the viewing period, have students look over their notes and choose one show in which they felt the actors did an exceptionally good job of communicating a wide range of emotions. Ask students to each write two or three paragraphs describing their reactions to the show and how the work of the actor or actors increased their enjoyment of the show. If there are students who don't feel that any of the shows they watched were exceptional, have them choose one show and explain what the actor or actors might have done differently to improve the show.

Art Critics at Work

Display a variety of prints of different styles of visual arts—paintings, collages, sculptures, and so on. Ask students to each select one piece to respond to as a critic. Their written critiques should tell what they liked or didn't like about the artist's work and why they felt as they did.

Artists' Autobiographies

Read aloud *A Very Young Musician,* by Jill Krementz (Simon and Schuster, 1991), or make the book available to interested students to read independently. This nonfiction book features a ten-year-old trumpet player. He describes how he got started, his lessons, practice sessions, and experiences that helped build his interest in music.

Invite interested students to create their own artistic autobiographies patterned after the book. Explain that they are not limited to music—their art may be drama, voice, dance, painting, drawing, sculpture, handicrafts, and so on. Encourage students to include photographs of themselves performing and practicing their art or illustrated examples of work they have created.

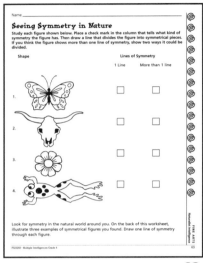

Naturalist Intelligence

Seeing Symmetry in Nature

Invite students to study the natural objects around them with the discerning eye of an artist. Can they spot examples of symmetry—figures that could be cut into two parts that would be reflections of one another? A butterfly, a flower, a human being—all are examples of symmetrical figures.

Discuss with students the different kinds of symmetry. A figure can have one line of symmetry. This means a line can be drawn only one way to divide the figure into symmetrical halves.

Some figures have multiple lines of symmetry. They can be divided into symmetrical halves in more than one way. A circle is an example. Divide it top to bottom and the two halves are symmetrical. Divide it from side to side at the middle and the same thing is true. A snowflake also has many lines of symmetry. You can draw a line almost anywhere to divide it into two halves that look the same.

Offer students copies of the **Seeing Symmetry in Nature** worksheet found on page 63. Have them follow the directions to complete the activities.

page 63

Natural Imagination

Ask students to let their minds wander and imagine what it would be like to be one of the following things from nature: a creature from the sea, a wild horse, a bird, a dinosaur, a seed sprouting into a plant, a cloud during a spring shower, a tree in a hurricane, or any other natural phenomenon. Have them write a short story to describe their new selves. Encourage them to use additional characters, conflict, resolution, dialogue, and other components of creative writing. To create a stimulating atmosphere for the activity, supply recordings of sounds from nature such as an ocean, animal, or rainstorm. Have students illustrate their work using paint, clay, or another medium.

Name _____

Puzzling Dimensions

Turn a two-dimensional object into a three-dimensional one with just a twist of the wrist! Follow the directions to make a Möbius strip, a mathematical puzzle that has inspired artists.

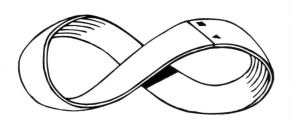

1. Cut out the strip at the right of the page. Study the rectangle you cut. It is a two-dimensional, or flat, figure.

2. Hold the strip in your hands, one hand at each end. Give one end a half twist, so the symbols on that end can no longer be seen as shown below.

3. Still holding both ends, bring them together so they butt up against one another. Tape the ends together. The same symbols will line up with each other, but they will be on opposite surfaces of the strip.

4. You have turned the two-dimensional rectangle into a three-dimensional Möbius strip. Now, with a pencil, draw a straight line down the middle of the strip lengthwise. You can start anywhere. What did you discover?

_____

_____

5. What do you predict will happen if you cut the strip along the line you just drew?

_____

_____

6. Carefully cut along the line. What happens?

_____

_____

Logical-Mathematical Intelligence

FINE ARTS

Name _____

Organizing the Orchestra

Musical instruments are put into different categories based on the method of producing sound. The list below will help you complete the activity.

String instruments: Sound is produced by vibrating a stretched string by plucking, striking, or using a bow.

Woodwind instruments: Sound is made by vibrating a reed.

Brass instruments: Sound is produced by blowing into a cup mouthpiece.

Percussion instruments: Sound is made by striking, tapping, or shaking.

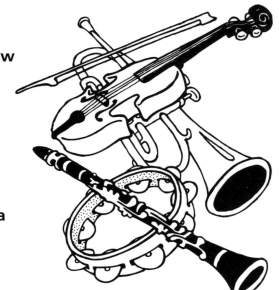

Organize the instruments listed below by putting each one into the correct section of the orchestra.

clarinet	French horn	triangle	bass
trumpet	piccolo	tambourine	snare drum
oboe	bassoon	cymbals	tuba
kettledrum	violin	xylophone	viola
trombone	cello	harp	English horn

String Section	Woodwind Section	Brass Section	Percussion Section

reproducible

Name _____

Seeing Symmetry in Nature

Study each figure shown below. Place a check mark in the column that tells what kind of symmetry the figure has. Then draw a line that divides the figure into symmetrical pieces. If you think the figure shows more than one line of symmetry, show two ways it could be divided.

Shape   **Lines of Symmetry**

                                    1 Line   **More than 1 line**

1.   ☐   ☐

2.   ☐   ☐

3.   ☐   ☐

4.   ☐   ☐

Look for symmetry in the natural world around you. On the back of this worksheet, illustrate three examples of symmetrical figures you found. Draw one line of symmetry through each figure.

FINE ARTS
Naturalist Intelligence

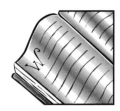

Verbal-Linguistic Intelligence

Sports Reporting

Invite students to act as sports journalists by writing an account of a school or professional sporting event they attended or watched on television. Remind them that the article must offer the information required by any news article: answers to the questions *who, what, when, where, how,* and *why.* Encourage students to add colorful headlines that feature action words.

Hero Reports

Encourage students to read about and report on an athlete who is accomplished in a sport the student enjoys as a participant or observer. Provide students with copies of the **Sports Hero** worksheet found on page 71. Have them use this form as the basis for their reports. Some suggested titles to use as references are listed below.

page 71

- *Babe Didrikson: Athlete of the Century,* by R.R. Knudson (Puffin, 1986)

- *Bicycle Rider,* by Mary Scioscia (HarperCollins, 1993)

- *Bo Jackson: Super Athlete,* by J. Spence (Lerner, 1991)

- *The Home Run Kings: Babe Ruth and Henry Aaron,* by Clare and Frank Gault (Scholastic, 1991)

- *Jackie Robinson and the Breaking of the Color Barrier,* by Russell Shorto (Millbrook Press, 1991)

- *Jesse Owens: Champion Athlete,* by Rick Rennert (Chelsea House, 1992)

- *Jim Abbot Against the Odds,* by Ellen Emerson White (Scholastic, 1990)

- *Michael Jordan,* by Chip Lovitt (Scholastic, 1993)

- *Pride of Puerto Rico: The Life of Roberto Clemente,* by Paul Robert Walker (Harcourt Brace, 1991)

- *Skating for the Gold,* by Chip Lovitt, about Tara Lipinski and Michelle Kwan (Scholastic, 1997)

· *Magic Johnson, Basketball Wizard,* by Martin Schwabacher (Chelsea House, 1995)

· *Wilma Rudolph: Champion Athlete,* by Victoria Sherrow (Chelsea House, 1995)

Logical-Mathematical Intelligence

Ball Patterns

Have students work in pairs to create and imitate patterns as they work with balls. Give each pair a small play ball. Have them work together for approximately five minutes to create a pattern of throwing, catching, and bouncing the ball. Remind them that creating a pattern means they must develop a sequence of movements that is repeated several times.

Put two or three pairs together to teach one another the patterns they developed. Then have the larger group develop a more intricate ball-handling pattern using two or three balls. Invite groups to teach these patterns to the rest of the class.

Testing Reaction Time

Have students work with partners to test one another's reaction time. Offer each pair a 12-inch ruler and a copy of the **Reaction Time** worksheet on page 72. (Do not use rulers with metal strips along an edge.)

Demonstrate the technique for dropping and catching the ruler. Hold the ruler in front of you with one hand. Drop it and catch it between the fingers of the other hand. Show students how to read the measurement closest to the point where you caught the ruler. Explain that the closer to the bottom the ruler is caught, the faster the reaction time is.

Have students follow the directions on the activity page as they test one another and record the results.

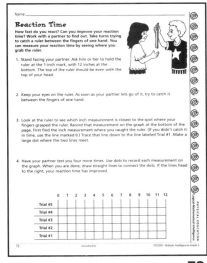

page 72

Olympic Lengths

Discuss the different lengths of Olympic track events. There are races at each of the following distances: 100, 200, 400, 800, 1500, 5000, and 10,000 meters. On the playground, have students mark a starting line and then measure off an oval, 100-meter course. Then ask them to compute how many laps would be required for each race and where each would end. Ask students to choose one of the shorter Olympic distances they would each like to run. Provide stopwatches and have them time their runs.

Bodily-Kinesthetic Intelligence

Playtime Sports Preparation

Activities that involve throwing, catching, kicking, and running build skills that students need when playing organized sports. At recess time, try some of the skill-builder activities described below.

Ball Volley: Mark two parallel lines about 20 feet apart. Divide the class into two equal teams. Team members stand behind the line on their team's side, except for one player, who will act as the first server. The server tosses a volleyball up slightly with one hand and hits it with the other, sending it toward the opposite team. If a member of that team can catch the ball before it hits the ground, he or she becomes the server. Otherwise, the first server takes another turn. Keep score for each team. Continue for a specified length of time.

Hot Ball: Players stand in a circle, facing inward. The designated starter places a soccer ball on the ground in front of him or her. The starter calls out, "Hot ball!" and kicks the ball across the circle, soccer style (using the inside of the foot). The player the ball is kicked toward quickly kicks the ball somewhere else. The object is to keep the "hot" ball moving as quickly as possible. Continue until the ball is kicked out of the circle. Then a new player can act as starter and set things in motion again.

Ball Rounds: Play this game on a hard surface. Have players form two equal teams, each with a designated leader. The teams form two large circles. Using both hands, the leader passes a basketball to the player on the right. As quickly as possible, the second player passes to the third, and so on until the ball returns to the leader. The leader then bounces the ball off the playground surface, toward the player on the right. That player catches the ball, then bounces it to the next person, who does the same. The game ends when the ball reaches the leader again. Check to see which team moves the ball fastest.

A-maze-ing Motor Skills

Provide students with opportunities to practice fine motor skills and eye-hand coordination as they create and solve mazes. Give each student a sheet of graph paper measured in 1/2 or 1/4 inch squares. Using the grid markings for guidelines, students can design intricate mazes. First have them use pencil to lightly outline the path they want their maze to take, being sure it is continuous from start to finish. Once they have a path determined, and Start and Finish labeled, they can add false turns and dead ends that branch off from the path. When these sections are planned out, students should outline all paths with marker or heavy pencil, then erase the light pencil line that traces the path through the maze. They can illustrate the surrounding sections to make their maze a trip through a swamp, outer space, or any other location they wish. Finished mazes can be reproduced and given to classmates to solve. Or mazes can be slipped into acetate folders and erasable markers can be used to trace a path.

Visual-Spatial Intelligence

Looking in the Mirror

Arrange students in pairs and explain that they are going to take turns acting as one another's reflection. Ask them to face their partners, standing with feet together and hands hanging down at their sides. Designate one student in each pair as the mirror and the other as the person looking in the mirror. The "looker" will initiate slow movements within a small area, with the "mirror" trying to copy those movements exactly. Have students practice by all trying the same movements first. For example, ask them to raise and lower one arm, slide one step sideways and back, and so on.

Then have students work independently with their partners, initiating and reflecting a series of movements. Halfway through the activity, have the "looker" and "mirror" switch jobs.

When students are finished, discuss the experience. How difficult did students find it to reflect their partners? Was it confusing at first to mirror an action using the opposite limb—for example, raising the left arm to reflect a partner's raising of the right arm?

Musical Intelligence

Musical Tag

Get students involved in a class game of musical tag. You will need a portable tape recorder and some lively music. On the playground, have students spread out in a large, open area. Choose a volunteer to be "it." Explain that you will be starting a recording. As the music plays, students should run within the designated boundaries of the play area. "It" can run as well, but can't tag anyone—until the moment the music stops. Start the music. After a minute or two, shut it off. Whoever "it" captures becomes the next "it."

In Step

Invite students to create marching units with a focus on performing drills in unison. First play marching music and have the class work together to practice basic moves such as marching in step to the music, turning, stopping, and so on. Stress the need to move in unison and in time with the music.

Then divide the class into drill teams, each eight to twelve members. Have the teams develop their own drills—patterns of movements they will do as they march to the music. After teams have had time to practice, have them demonstrate their drills for one another.

Interpersonal Intelligence

Fitness Follow the Leader

In the school gymnasium or on the playground, demonstrate a Follow the Leader game that focuses on fitness activities. For example, you might run one lap around the gym, do five jumping jacks, hop on one foot twice, and do ten sit-ups. Choose a student to act as leader after you. To give many students the opportunity to act as leader, you may want to limit each leader to a sequence of four or five activities before a new leader is chosen. Stress that leaders should not model any activity that might be unsafe for others in the group.

Pathway Partners

Set up a "pathway" on the classroom or hallway floor. It should include at least one turn. With masking tape, outline both sides of a path about 18 inches wide by 8 feet long. Have students line up at one end of the path and then walk single file along it, being very careful not to step out of the lines.

Then explain that they are each going to walk the path again, but this time it won't be so easy because they will be blindfolded. They will have to depend on a partner to provide them with the clues their eyes had given them the first time they walked the path.

Have students select partners. Choose a pair to go first, with one student acting as the blindfolded walker and the other as a guide. The guide can quietly say "right" or "left" to tell the walker which way to go to avoid stepping off the path. If his partner does step completely off the path, the guide has to tell him to stop and then use direction words to get him back on the path. After the walker makes it all the way down the path, the two change places.

When one pair finishes their walk, they should send another pair to the path. After all students have had a chance to try to navigate the path without visual cues, have a class discussion about the experience.

Intrapersonal Intelligence

Heart Rate Activities

Challenge students to perform certain activities that will raise their heart rate. After they perform the activities listed on the worksheet on page 73, **Target Your Heart**, they should check their heart rates and record them on the same sheet. There is a chart at the top of the sheet that will help students to know if they are within their target heart rate.

Relaxation Time

At the end of an intense activity, provide time for students to relax—literally. Explain that relaxation doesn't mean taking it easy or being lazy. It means letting go of tension in a muscle or group of muscles. Knowing how to relax is important both mentally and physically.

Have students sit comfortably in their chairs or on the floor. Ask them to each hold out one arm and tense the muscles. Have them use the opposite hand to feel the muscles in the tensed arm. Then, while still feeling the muscle, ask them to relax the arm. Discuss the differences they perceive between the tensed and relaxed muscle.

Try some relaxation exercises. Ask students to imagine the following scenarios:

- You are a snowman on a hot day. You are melting...melting...melting...
- You are a balloon that is getting bigger and bigger. And then—you burst.
- Suddenly you have no backbone.
- You are a sail caught in the wind—and then the wind dies down.

At the end of the exercise, discuss with students how they might use similar techniques when they feel a need to relax. Help them understand that being able to consciously relax tensed muscles can reduce mental tension.

Personal Fitness Goals

Encourage students to identify and work toward achieving a set of personal fitness goals. First discuss the different aspects of physical fitness as described below:

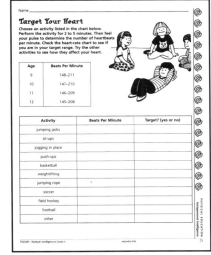

page 73

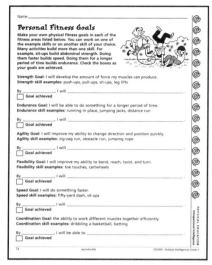

page 74

Strength: the amount of force a particular muscle can exert.

Endurance: the ability to maintain an activity over a period of time.

Agility: the ability to change direction or position quickly and with control.

Flexibility: the ability to bend, reach, twist, and turn.

Power: using the maximum amount of force in the shortest time possible.

Speed: the ability to repeat patterns of movements rapidly.

Balance: the ability to hold a body position steadily.

Coordination: the ability to work different muscles together efficiently.

Offer students copies of the **Personal Fitness Goals** worksheet found on page 74. Encourage them to record their own goals in each aspect of physical fitness listed there. After several weeks, have them reread their goals and reflect upon which goals have been met and whether any need to be revised.

Naturalist Intelligence

Outdoors Projects

Have students create a personal project based on an outdoor activity that they enjoy doing on their own. Some activities to choose from are: hiking, fishing, camping, bird watching, cross-county running, skiing. Have the students create a list of goals they'd like to meet in this activity. (Parental supervision will be needed for some activities.) Students can also include any of the following in their project: safety tips for the sports or activity, instructions on how to perform a task or skill related to the activity, a map, a photo essay, or a journal. Have students present their reports to the class.

Healthy Students, Healthy Earth

Students can improve their own health through physical exercise while caring for the world around them. Have students commit to a clean-up day in the school yard or nearby park by picking up trash; planting, watering, and feeding plants; raking or clearing trails. Enlist the help of the maintenance department or rangers and keep safety in mind. For example, gloves should be worn to pick up trash. Also, observe the rules of the park or preserve by staying on trails, for example, and not trampling plants.

Sports Hero

Use this form to report on an athlete you consider a hero.

Name of athlete: _____

_____

Date of birth: _____

Nationality: _____

The athlete's sport or sports: _____

Major accomplishments: _____

_____

_____

_____

Obstacles the athlete had to overcome: _____

_____

_____

_____

Why I admire this athlete: _____

_____

_____

Books or magazine articles I have read about this athlete: _____

_____

_____

_____

CHAMPION

PHYSICAL EDUCATION
Verbal-Linguistic Intelligence

Reaction Time

How fast do you react? Can you improve your reaction time? Work with a partner to find out. Take turns trying to catch a ruler between the fingers of one hand. You can measure your reaction time by seeing where you grab the ruler.

1. Stand facing your partner. Ask him or her to hold the ruler at the 1-inch mark, with 12 inches at the bottom. The top of the ruler should be even with the top of your head.

2. Keep your eyes on the ruler. As soon as your partner lets go of it, try to catch it between the fingers of one hand.

3. Look at the ruler to see which inch measurement is closest to the spot where your fingers grasped the ruler. Record that measurement on the graph at the bottom of the page. First find the inch measurement where you caught the ruler. (If you didn't catch it in time, use the line marked 0.) Trace that line down to the line labeled Trial #1. Make a large dot where the two lines meet.

4. Have your partner test you four more times. Use dots to record each measurement on the graph. When you are done, draw straight lines to connect the dots. If the lines head to the right, your reaction time has improved.

	0	1	2	3	4	5	6	7	8	9	10	11	12
Trial #5													
Trial #4													
Trial #3													
Trial #2													
Trial #1													

PHYSICAL EDUCATION Logical-Mathematical Intelligence

Target Your Heart

Choose an activity listed in the chart below. Perform the activity for 2 to 5 minutes. Then feel your pulse to determine the number of heartbeats per minute. Check the heart-rate chart to see if you are in your target range. Try the other activities to see how they affect your heart.

Age	Beats Per Minute
9	148–211
10	147–210
11	146–209
12	145–208

Activity	Beats Per Minute	Target? (yes or no)
jumping jacks		
sit-ups		
jogging in place		
push-ups		
basketball		
weightlifting		
jumping rope		
soccer		
field hockey		
football		
other		

PHYSICAL EDUCATION
Intrapersonal Intelligence

Personal Fitness Goals

Make your own physical fitness goals in each of the fitness areas listed below. You can work on one of the example skills or on another skill of your choice. Many activities build more than one skill. For example, sit-ups build abdominal strength. Doing them faster builds speed. Doing them for a longer period of time builds endurance. Check the boxes as your goals are achieved.

Strength Goal: I will develop the amount of force my muscles can produce.
Strength skill examples: push-ups, pull-ups, sit-ups, leg lifts

By _____, I will _____ .
☐ **Goal achieved**

Endurance Goal: I will be able to do something for a longer period of time.
Endurance skill examples: running in place, jumping jacks, distance run

By _____, I will _____ .
☐ **Goal achieved**

Agility Goal: I will improve my ability to change direction and position quickly.
Agility skill examples: zig-zag run, obstacle run, jumping rope

By _____, I will _____ .
☐ **Goal achieved**

Flexibility Goal: I will improve my ability to bend, reach, twist, and turn.
Flexibility skill examples: toe touches, cartwheels

By _____, I will _____ .
☐ **Goal achieved**

Speed Goal: I will do something faster.
Speed skill examples: fifty-yard dash, sit-ups

By _____, I will _____ .
☐ **Goal achieved**

Coordination Goal: the ability to work different muscles together efficiently.
Coordination skill examples: dribbling a basketball, batting

By _____, I will be able to _____ .
☐ **Goal achieved**

Page 28 Exploring for Explorers

1. Portuguese
2. Christopher Columbus
3. Italian
4. Vasco da Gama
5. First European to see Pacific Ocean
6. Ponce de León
7. Conquered Mexico
8. Francisco Pizzaro
9. Spanish
10. French
11. First European to discover Hudson Bay and River
12. Louis Joliet and Jaques Marquette
13. Explored east coast of Australia
14. Explored the Louisiana Territory
15. Canadian
16. Sir William Parry
17. American
18. Explored Africa
19. Led first expedition to reach North Pole
20. Roald Amundsen

Page 40 Mystery Equations

1. $(24 \div 3) - 1 = 7$ or $8 - 1 = 7$
2. $65 - (2 \times 6) = 53$ or $65 - 12 = 53$
3. $400 \div (8 \times 5) = 10$ or $400 \div 40 = 10$
4. $(103 + 23) - 100 = 26$ or $126 - 100 = 26$
5. $6 \times (2 + 4) = 36$ or $6 \times 6 = 36$
6. $(22 + 101) \times 0 = 0$ or $123 \times 0 = 0$
7. $(42 \div 7) + (21 \div 3) = 13$ or $6 + 7 = 13$
8. $(6 \times 0) + (12 \times 3) = 36$ or $0 + 36 = 36$
9. $(4 + 4) + (6 \times 6) = 44$ or $8 + 36 = 44$
10. $(6 \div 3) + (6 - 3) + (6 + 3) = 14$; or $2 + 3 + 9 = 14$
11. $(100 \div 10) \times (50 \div 10) = 50$ or $10 \times 5 = 50$
12. $(3 \times 4) + (5 + 6) + (8 - 7) = 24$ or $12 + 11 + 1 = 24$

Page 41 Pascal's Triangle

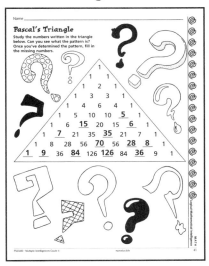

Page 52 Science Analogies

1. quartz; Sandstone is a kind of sedimentary rock. Quartz is a kind of metamorphic rock.
2. toad; Rattlesnake and alligator belong to the same animal family. A toad and a salamander are in the same family.
3. acacia; Pandas eat bamboo. Giraffes eat acacia.
4. dinosaur; Astrology is the study of stars and paleontology is the study of dinosaurs.
5. heart; The lungs control respiration, and the heart controls circulation.
6. monkey; A snake is a cold-blooded animal. A monkey is a warm-blooded animal.
7. Pluto; Mercury and Venus are inner planets. Uranus and Pluto are outer planets.
8. ice; An avalanche is moving snow. A glacier is moving ice.
9. penicillin; Curie discovered radium. Fleming discovered penicillin.
10. liter; Centimeter and inch are metric and standard measurements of length. Liter and quart are metric and standard measurements for volume.

Page 54 Food Web

Page 62 Organizing the Orchestra
Strings: bass; violin; viola; cello; harp.
Woodwinds: clarinet; piccolo; oboe; bassoon;
English horn.
Brass: French horn; trumpet; tuba; trombone.
Percussion: triangle; tambourine; snare drum;
cymbals; kettledrum; xylophone

Page 63 Seeing Symmetry in Nature
1. 1 line of symmetry
2. 1 line of symmetry
3. more than 1 line of symmetry
4. 1 line of symmetry